by Cynthia Kreuger

BRIGHTON PUBLICATIONS, INC.

Brighton Publications, Inc.
PO Box 120706
St. Paul, MN 55112-0706
(651)636-2220

First Edition: 1993

Library of Congress Cataloging-in-Publication Data

Kreuger, Cynthia
    Dream weddings do come true : how to plan a stress-free wedding / by Cynthia Kreuger.
        p. cm.
    Includes index.
    1. Weddings—United States—Planning. 2. Stress (Psychology) 3. Marriage customs and rites—United States.
I. Title.
HQ745.K73 1993   92-34155
395'.22—dc20   CIP
        ISBN 0-918420-18-0

Printed in the United States of America

*To my mentor who taught
me to follow my dreams.*

ℰontents

Introduction   9

Chapter 1: The Art of Becoming Engaged   13

Contemplating Marriage   13
Informing Parents   18
Sharing the News   22
Newspaper Announcement   25

Chapter 2: Engagement Issues   27

Recognizing Behavioral Patterns   27
Surfacing Emotions   28
Dealing with Disapproval   32
Blending Values   36
What to Call In-laws   40
A Changing Phase   41

Chapter 3: From Dream Wedding to Reality   42

Visualize Your Wedding   42
Parental Participation   46
Hidden Agendas   46
Who Pays   47
Controlling Decisions   50
Compromising   54

Chapter 4: Who Will Attend   55

  Choosing Attendants   55
  Inviting Guests   58
  Children: Yes or No   61
  Accommodating Guests   65

Chapter 5: Selecting Suppliers   69

  How to Find   69
  Record Keeping   72
  Before Signing the Contract   73
  Dot the i's and Cross the t's   76
  When to Rely on the Supplier   77
  Use Your Creativity   81

Chapter 6: Specific Supplier Solutions   87

  Ceremony and Reception   87
  Photographer and Videographer   94
  The Wedding Gown   97
  Florist   99
  Music   101
  Bridal Consultant   103
  Invitations   104
  Wedding Cake   106
  Tuxedos   107
  Transportation   107

Chapter 7: Planning the Ceremony   110

  Religious Influence   110
  Locating a Facility   112
  Complying with Religious Rules   114
  Interfaith Marriage   116
  Designing the Ceremony   117
  The Processional   118

A Welcome Prayer   119
Choosing the Officiant   120
Music, Readings, and Prayers   121
Encouraging Participation   124
Exchanging Vows   125
The Closing Elements   126
Receiving the Guests   126
Wedding Program   127
Divorced Parents   128
Consider the Children   129

Chapter 8: Planning the Reception   131

What Kind   131
Selecting Music   133
Menu Planning   135
How Formal?   137
Seating Plans   139
Introductions   139
Toasting   141
Special Moments   141
Couple's Departure   143

Chapter 9: Tension Areas   145

Negative Emotions   145
Why Jealousy?   147
Divorced Parents   149
Budget   150
Choice of Residence   153
How Children Fit In   155
Insecurity   155
Handling Frustration   156

Chapter 10: Dealing with Stress   158

    The Causes of Stress   158
    The Nature of Stress   159
    Physical Reasons for Stress   160
    Demands   161
    Conquering Fear   166
    Decreasing Stress   168
    Asserting One's Self   169
    Building Self-esteem   170
    Express Yourself   171

Chapter 11: Learning to Communicate   172

    How You See Yourself   172
    Understanding Conversation   173
    Response Awareness   175
    Choosing the Right Words   175
    Don't Assume   177
    Controlling Arguments   179
    The Nagging Parent Within   181
    Respecting the Private Self   181
    Marriage Help   183

Afterthought   185

Index   187

$\mathcal{I}$ntroduction

Best wishes as you become engaged and begin to design your special day! The journey to your new life holds challenges, but as you follow this book's real-life solutions, a direction for your wedding will unfold making your engagement a time of excitement, romance, and love. You can bask in the pleasure of the experience, while making a commitment to have one of the most fulfilling times of your lives.

Working as a bridal consultant, I have met couples who have encountered and successfully negotiated the steps leading to their ceremonies and receptions. You will find stories of their dreams and how they turned their dreams into realities in this book. On the way to their celebrations the couples gained skills necessary to orchestrate story-book perfect weddings and prepare for successful marriages.

In my career I witness the pain of young women unable to assert their desires, and I experience their joy as they learn it's all right to express personal needs to their fiancés and families. I see young couples learn to express their requirements to professional business representatives and achieve positive results. I observe couples making a commitment to unite in their life endeavors.

These are people with lives similar to yours. The solutions they found to their problems may become your own, and their experiences may contain the answers to your dilemmas. The lessons they learned can support you in meeting your challenges.

One of the main points the couples have to share is that your wedding will be as perfect as you allow it to be. One bride and groom achieved perfection in their special day even though various decisions were changed and compromises with parents and suppliers became necessary during the wedding planning stages. On their wedding day, the organist changed the processional music because she forgot the sheet music the bride had chosen. The florist forgot the ring bearer's boutonniere and the bridal consultant needed to make one from part of a bridesmaid's bouquet. The banquet hall refused to provide glasses of water because the beverage was not on the contract. The father-of-the-bride needed to pay for the service in order to accommodate the guests.

During all of the disruptions, the bride and groom were able to focus on their joy and find pleasure in the many events that were perfect during their wedding.

Perception will work against you if you allow it. The groom who can focus on nothing but the scratchy shirt provided by the formalwear shop, and the bride who is angry that the hue of the ribbons on the bridesmaids' bouquets is slightly different from their gowns create their own negative experience. She knew the florist would goof, and she fills her mind with her displeasure.

The two are dissatisfied and ill-tempered on their wedding day. While the guests perceived the ceremony as splendid, the reception food as excellent, and the band as enjoyable, the bride and groom had a miserable day.

Your wedding may be the first major party you have planned. Organizing the ceremony and reception requires that you decide what it is you wish to achieve, present the organized plan to your parents, and then locate and contract the appropriate wedding suppliers.

There will be numerous tasks to perform and decisions to make, but they can be dealt with easily and efficiently if you know what you want, communicate your needs to one another and the wedding suppliers, and remain in control of your thoughts and plans.

Anticipating the perplexity with which couples face wedding strategies and emotional stresses of major life changes, this book offers you explanations from real-life examples and common sense solutions to your questions.

Provided here are instructions for developing a dream wedding, procedures for choosing attendants and selecting suppliers, plans for a personalized ceremony and successful reception, and assistance in developing skills required to minimize stress and maximize effective communication.

There are ideas for blending the three distinct family units—the bride and groom, the bride's family, and the groom's family—into a harmonious and nurturing association.

You are in the process of becoming married, a major event which will influence all other aspects of your lives. The values, belief systems, and habits you have learned from your families are the same as those you will bring to your marriage. Your engagement is an ideal time to explore various behaviors which are mutually empowering as well as those which conflict. Behaviors which strengthen your relationship can be nurtured and those that weaken the relationship may be modified in order to create a harmonious, loving, and sustaining marriage.

Your engagement is an opportunity to establish mutual goals of your ideal wedding and a loving, supportive marriage. This is the time to begin learning to discuss important issues with one another and work toward the achievement of your desires and resolution of your difficulties.

There are a number of skills offered here which will allow you to attain your dream wedding while developing your individual potential. Negotiation skills, stress-management, communication skills, conflict resolution, and the elimination of limiting habits are among the benefits which can be gained by learning from the engagement experience.

We are constantly in a state of becoming our best. Preparing for life events, such as a wedding, allows quality experiences for personal growth. Through bridal consulting and wedding planning workshops, I have enjoyed watching many men and women develop their potential as they worked toward their wedding day and achieve a wedding they could truly call perfect for them.

Andrew and Linda learned to talk with one another about their dreams for the wedding before they tried to negotiate their desires with numerous wedding suppliers.

Faith explored what it meant to leave her family and begin a new life with Rod as she wrote her thoughts for her wedding program.

Maria learned to say what she needed rather than have others guess her wedding requirements.

Tracy learned that he and his mother had a more satisfying relationship when he was allowed to be himself rather than pretend he was his brother's mirror image.

Jill learned to transact business with wedding suppliers who had been operating their services for numerous years. An achievement Jill thought she never would attain.

Each time an individual took action to change a limiting behavior, he or she also became more successful as part of a couple. You bring all of your behaviors to your marriage, and the better you can be for yourself, the more your relationship improves.

As a bridal consultant I've learned how the engagement period can become an opportunity for personal growth. The tasks associated with planning a wedding can be difficult. Coping with changing relationships can be an issue, too. But when you manage the stress, your reward will be the realization of a dream wedding.

Keep in touch with what you are experiencing and learn from each phase of your engagement. This is a dynamic time in your life, and you can make it the best. With the many ideas and true-life stories offered here, you can develop your dream and make it come true. I wish for you the best life has to offer. Enjoy the process!

1

The Art of Becoming Engaged

An engagement is a period of time leading to the establishment of a long-term relationship built on love and respect. How the engagement begins, it's length, and what occurs during this time is unique to each couple. Many conflicts and crises will be experienced during this time. How they are resolved will provide building blocks to a successful marriage.

Usually during this engagement, the man and woman adjust to not only being a couple, but a part of an extended family. The engagement, the wedding, and the couple's future are planned and discussed with parents and friends.

New alliances are formed and old relationships end as the couple spend more time pursuing mutual interests with people who relate to them as a pair. Each becomes an insider to the other's family unit, and in the process learns the expectations and interactions of those family members.

Contemplating Marriage

The days of a man becoming betrothed on bended knee while in the presence of a chaperone have long passed. Today's couples are more sophisticated about their impending marriages. Many have already shared a household together and some have been married before. Most have discussed their desires for a future life together and have reached a joint decision to marry.

Family and friends often assume that a couple are destined for matrimony before the engagement is official. On occasion, well-meaning friends make pointed comments to the couple which may influence a hasty decision to marry, or raise doubts about how well-matched the couple might be. In any event, traditional, formal proposals are no longer the norm.

Sarah and Ron had been dating for two years before Sarah's summer vacation in Europe. The vacation was a graduation present from her parents, and Sarah was thrilled with the prospect of international travel. Ron had graduated a year prior to Sarah and was already establishing his career. During the past six months, they had been discussing the possibility of spending the rest of their lives together. They discussed where they'd like to live, how their two careers could complement each other, how many children they'd like to have, and what their expectations were for the future.

Relatives and friends began to treat Sarah and Ron as a couple. Invitations were extended to both of them. Family celebrations and holidays were shared jointly. Those persons close to Sarah and Ron expected they would marry.

Sarah left for Europe, knowing the time apart would be difficult, but that her travels would enrich her. Ron counted the days until Sarah's return. While Sarah was away, Ron discussed an engagement with her parents. He told them that he'd purchased a diamond ring to give to Sarah at the airport. Her parents assured Ron that they were pleased and knew Sarah would accept his proposal.

At the airport, Ron and Sarah greeted each other as lovers do after an extended separation. On the way to the baggage area, Ron pulled Sarah into a coin-operated photo booth. She laughed, remembering the numerous times they had taken funny pictures of themselves in photo booths. Before the camera snapped, Ron reached into his pocket and produced a small box. He removed the ring, and captured his proposal to Sarah on film.

Upon their return to her home, Sarah and Ron announced their engagement and then calmly made an appointment with Sarah's parents to have dinner and discuss their future plans.

Sarah and Ron had established a solid foundation that progressed their relationship naturally (yet very romantically) to the engagement. Others are more impulsive, which can create its own kind of stress.

Kimberly had spent the year in France as an exchange student, during which time she and Jean Paul had fallen hopelessly in love. Jean Paul's English was lacking, but Kimberly's French was fluent.

As Kimberly's term ended, she and Jean Paul grew uneasy about her departure. They had spent numerous hours talking about those activities which gave each of them pleasure, and they discussed what each hoped to accomplish in his lifetime. They also reflected on the growth of their friendship and their compatibility, but never did they discuss an engagement. It seemed too difficult to imagine being apart, but also too difficult to construct a life together from their diverse backgrounds. To them, silence seemed their best solution.

Kimberly did leave France that summer and sadly returned to her parent's home. The days seemed to drag on for her, and it seemed all she had to look forward to were the letters Jean Paul wrote faithfully, and the phone calls he sometimes made to her.

One particular day, Kimberly received a call from Jean Paul telling her he was making a trip to the U.S. and, without Kimberly's knowledge, Jean Paul also spoke with her parents, and made arrangements to meet privately with her father on the day of Jean Paul's arrival in America.

While Jean Paul's ability to communicate in English was limited, he had rehearsed what he wished to say to Kimberly's father. He asked for permission to marry Kimberly and take her back to France with him. Kimberly's father was surprised at the request and asked if Kimberly was aware of Jean Paul's plans. She was not. Her father then stated that Jean Paul and Kimberly should discuss their future together, and that he and Kimberly's mother would abide by the couple's decision.

Kimberly and Jean Paul had many details to negotiate. Two different cultural backgrounds, two different homelands, and two different languages were only their first obstacles. They were young, and Kimberly still had one year of college to finish. It now seemed as if the year in France had been wasted as far as discussing their future together. But at least they had shared many of their feelings, values, and dreams during their long talks in France.

Kimberly and Jean Paul did eventually marry. Much of Jean Paul's family, and even his priest, made the journey to the United States for the wedding ceremony.

Kimberly is finishing her last year of college in France and Jean Paul is working on his master's degree. They are content living in his homeland now, but plan to eventually reside in America.

Dating in France, Jean Paul and Kimberly missed

the opportunity to discuss and negotiate possible stress points in their marriage. The primary opportunity to explore and modify behaviors which conflict occurs before marriage. Many of Kimberly and Jean Paul's obstacles were obvious because of the different nationalities, but all couples have differences which need to be identified and discussed.

Kimberly's parents were her sole financial support, but today that is not the norm. Parents are unlikely to be the sole financial support of their young adult children today. As a result of this new freedom, couples may choose to accept or ignore parental wishes. The emotional support of a parent, however, is always a factor in an individual's life and, even today, many parents may choose to withhold their support at this most meaningful and stressful time.

There are times when parents view obstacles to their children's future happiness as insurmountable, and they are reluctant to give approval to the marriage. Other parents may hold prejudices or hostilities toward their children's plans.

Molly's heritage is Irish, and while she knows the pride her parents take in that heritage, she feels no ties to the native land of her grandparents.

Molly, a graduate of Notre Dame like many of her relatives, began her career as a civil engineer. During one of her on-site tours, she met Frank, a Mexican-American, blue collar worker.

Today, she confesses that she's not sure why she was first attracted to Frank. Although she finds him quite friendly and attractive, she thinks it may be the diversity of their backgrounds which first appealed to her.

As their friendship began, Molly's parents refused to allow Frank to escort their daughter to family functions. When friendship turned to love and an engagement was announced, the reluctance on the part of Molly's parents turned to open hostility.

The constant quarrels between Molly and her mother escalated to the point that Molly moved out of her parent's home to her own apartment. When she secured her own residence, her father stopped talking with Molly completely.

Determined to make a life together, in spite of Molly's parents, Frank and Molly eloped six months after their initial meeting and found themselves totally alienated from Molly's family.

Viewing her life now, Molly realizes that she accomplished little by the haste with which she promised to marry. She and Frank had a brief engagement period, with little discussion about their future. Molly was so enmeshed in her own family battles, she didn't take time to acquaint herself with Frank's family. Doing so would have given her an idea of Frank's expectations for marriage and family life, and would have given them groundwork on which to build.

Informing Parents

Once the decision to marry has been made, the couple should approach the bride-to-be's parents first, in part to gain their approval and guidance. Should her parents be divorced, the persons who raised her are initially informed. The couple may choose a location allowing them the most comfort. A favorite restaurant, their own apartment, or maybe the home of the bride's parents. Enough time needs to be scheduled into the meeting to discuss the initial plans for the wedding, and also the couple's expectations for the future.

Parents have both an emotional and financial stake in the wedding and the marriage. They will want to hear the plans the couple have made, as well as offer their suggestions and desires for the future of their daughter and son-in-law.

Initially, the bride's parents will probably have numerous questions about the wedding itself. If they are expected to pay for the majority of the wedding costs, there is even more reason for them to know how elaborate an affair the couple hope to have and when the event will occur.

As those first questions are resolved, the discussion often turns to more significant issues, such as the couple's ability to support themselves, the residence they hope to occupy, how they will maintain their careers, and their expectations for children.

Denise and David are firm believers in goal-setting for every aspect of their lives. During the three years they dated, they set benchmarks along the way. They moved toward his graduation as a graphic artist, and his acceptance of a position in a major firm. She worked as a secretary, gaining the business knowledge she would eventually require for their own graphic art company.

They knew exactly how much of their earnings needed to be deposited regularly in the bank account in order to have a down payment on a small home. A subdivision of the city was chosen where similar homes had been built. The couple knew a home would be available at any point in time. The particular style of home was chosen because it could be purchased cheaply and easily expanded in the future.

The couple determined when they would have children by calculating the income required to add a third person to their household, followed by two more youngsters.

When Denise and David had achieved their financial goal for the home, the engagement was announced. Denise's parents were invited to a favorite restaurant and informed of the couple's intention to marry.

Of course, the engagement was no surprise to Denise's parents, who had known for some time that their daughter was going to marry David. Her parents had been making financial plans of their own to pay for the wedding.

Denise's parents provided a budget within which they would need to work. Ideas were exchanged as to the formality of the wedding and the number of guests to be invited.

The bride and groom outlined their plans for the future, and her parents were assured that the two were well on their way to a successful and loving marriage.

Few couples have their lives as organized as Denise and David, but most realize there are a great number of issues to face during the engagement. On becoming engaged the couple begins the task of blending two different family styles. Often families have different rules for living and different expectations for what makes a marriage successful. They may harbor different ideas as to what is required for a comfortable existence, or the type of life they will design for themselves and their own children.

It is beneficial for the couple to take time to discuss expectations for the future and then present those ideas to their parents.

Once the bride's parents have become aware of the engagement, a similar meeting should be established with the parents of the groom-to-be. Allow the time to review with the groom's parents the discussion between the couple and the parents of the bride. Briefly sketch the wedding plans and listen to their desires for the wedding. Then in detail, explain the plans for the marriage. Allow the groom's parents time to ask questions and offer suggestions.

As a result of the meetings with the parents, the couple will be articulating a clearer image of their future, as well as opening a communication channel to discuss a vast number of issues in the months ahead.

If the parents of the bride and the parents of the groom have never met, now is the time for them to become acquainted. It is traditional for the groom's parents to issue the invitation to the bride's parents. The parents may include the couple in this meeting, but the option exists for the four parents to meet alone.

The parents of the groom may determine where this meeting will be most enjoyable, and then invite the bride's parents to their home, country club, a restaurant, or general meeting place.

If the groom's parents are unaware of this etiquette and fail to issue an invitation to the parents of the bride, her parents may establish the meeting, or the couple may take the initiative themselves.

This is meant to be a pleasant social occasion, rather than a planning session. Let the purpose of the meeting be the acquaintance of these key persons.

If the parents are already acquainted, it is still appropriate for the groom's parents to extend an invitation to the parents of the bride for a time of amiable and light friendly conversation.

This wonderful opportunity for increased friendship is lost to those parents of the couple who live a distance apart. Special effort is required to keep the lines of communication open in these circumstances. As with the social invitation, it is normally the parents of the groom who make the initial contact. A personal note to the parents of the bride is appropriate.

Once the etiquette requirements have been observed, parents will be directly informed about the couple's desire to marry, the couple's future will be outlined, and hopefully, the approval of the parents will be forthcoming.

In the case of a couple where one or both sets of parents are divorced, often one of the divorced parents has been excluded from the ritual of meeting the future in-laws. The bride and groom need to make a personal visit to recap the discussions which have already taken place with the other parents. Whatever the quality of involvement has been with this parent in the recent past, it must be understood that this member, too, has an emotional investment in the marriage.

Sharing the News

The news of the engagement may now be made public. The bride-to-be will wear her engagement ring proudly, and the couple inform siblings, other relations, co-workers, and friends of the engagement.

The bride's parents, or possibly the groom's parents, may request that the engagement be announced at a party in the couple's honor. The announcement can be made at whatever type of social gathering the hosts deem appropriate. It is often a party which suits the style of the guests of honor, such as a cocktail party, backyard barbeque, or an elegant sit-down dinner.

Nancy and Ron met at the local park district swimming pool where they both worked as life-guards during their summer vacations. The two enjoyed each other's company, and attended several events together during the week after the pool closed for the season.

Their friendship grew, and once they returned to their respective schools, they continued to pursue their relationship. They corresponded throughout the school year, and got together whenever they were both home on school break, or traveled to one another's school events.

The second summer together, Ron declared his love, and the two began to set their sights on marriage after graduation. Ron presented Nancy with a diamond ring at the close of the school year, and they informed her parents of their intention to marry.

Nancy's parents planned a pool party to celebrate and announce the engagement. The local pool, where the couple had met, was reserved for late Saturday night.

The pool was decorated to indicate the couple's lifestyle. A blow-up photo of the couple was taped to each of the lifeguard positions. An arch of balloons sailed over the center of the pool, with balloons sculpted into the shapes of a bride and groom in the middle.

The swim trophies and awards each had won were on display at the beverage table, and cartoon fish and mermaids were on the plates and napkins. Travel posters depicting water activities were posted on the walls and fences.

The appetizers also carried the theme, as bagels became life preservers, pineapples became boats, and mini-pizzas were cut in the shape of sea shells. There were fish crackers for the mini-mugs of clam chowder.

Nancy wore her ring, and of course, her parents had the band announce the engagement as the couple danced to their favorite song.

The couple out of courtesy, may wish to inform close family members and friends of the engagement before it becomes public knowledge. A personal visit, a phone call, or a short note of announcement, where distance is a factor, is a friendly gesture on the part of the couple.

If one of the two has been married before, another issue comes to the forefront. Children of the previous marriage have a tremendous emotional stake in the new union. They need to be informed long before the engagement that the possibility of a marriage exists, in order that a relationship can develop between the children and the future stepparent.

News of the engagement should come from no one other than the parent of the child. This is not a time to ask permission, but to allow the child to express his feelings about the new family which will be created.

Chuck and Karen had been dating for just over a year. During their courtship, Karen's daughter, Kimmy, was included in a great number of their outings. As time went on, Kimmy was invited, along with Karen, to Chuck's parents home for dinner, to his sister's for her children's birthday parties, and was generally accepted as part of the family.

The three of them discussed the possibility of marriage, and Kimmy, now eight years old, was very comfortable with the idea. Though she loved her father dearly, she accepted Chuck as a friend.

One evening, when Karen and Chuck were leaving Kimmy with her father, Chuck planned a special dinner for two at his apartment. He had a perfect gourmet dinner, candlelight, and soft music. Dessert was presented along with a diamond engagement ring.

The following day, Chuck and Karen planned to pick Kimmy up from her father and have an outing to the zoo. Chuck asked if they could take Kimmy to her favorite fast-food restaurant, after the zoo.

Completing an enjoyable, yet tiring, outing, the three stepped to the counter where Chuck ordered food for Karen and himself and then said he required the special meal-box for his youngest date. As pre-arranged, the cashier handed Chuck the labeled box, and it was passed along to Kimmy.

At the table, Kimmy searched her food box for the anticipated toy, but found instead a small jewelry box. Inside was a tiny diamond chip ring on a fine gold chain. Chuck told Kimmy he would like to start a special family.

After Karen and Kimmy were home alone, Karen showed Kimmy that she too had received a ring and a proposal of marriage. The two of them privately discussed their feelings about the new family unit, and what that might mean for Kimmy's relationship to her own father.

An ex-spouse also needs to be directly informed of the engagement. This is especially true when there is joint custody of the children. It will be necessary to spend time discussing the location of the new residence and how the parents can continue to share time with their children.

Newspaper Announcement

When close relatives and friends have been informed of the engagement, it is appropriate to make an announcement in the local newspaper. Announcements may be made as much as a year or more or as little as a week in advance of the wedding. On average, the announcement is made two to three months prior to the event.

The bride's parents most often make the engagement announcement, but other approaches are appropriate and acceptable. In the past, when an engagement photo was displayed, it was of the bride-to-be. Trends have changed in that it is now the norm to have a photo of the couple.

The announcement lists the names and city of the parents of the bride, the bride's name, the name of the man she is to marry, and his parents and city. Individual background information on the bride and groom is often included, such as high school, college, degrees earned, present employment. The information concludes with the wedding date and location.

It is wise not to alert the general public to the exact date of the wedding, because the announcement is a clear indication that the residence will be vacant on the day of the wedding. Listing the month and year of the event is sufficient.

Most newspapers print engagement announcements without charge. It is best to contact each individual paper for policy and requirements.

2
*E*ngagement
*I*ssues

The period between the promise to marry and the wedding day is an emotionally charged time for the couple, their families, and friends. There may never be another time in their lives when so many people have an emotional stake in so many decisions which the couple must make.

The engagement period may be demanding, but it is also a time of development and discovery in learning to live as adults within marriage and the couple's community. Effective communication and negotiation skills can be acquired, along with the ability to compromise during the decision making process.

For the more mature, the engagement period is one during which effective skills already acquired can be used and new skills developed. For the younger, less experienced couple the opportunity exists to learn new skills.

Recognizing Behavioral Patterns
Most people have learned how to relate to each other as husband and wife from their parents' example. As adults enter marriage, they have already

formed expectations as to how they should be treated and how they should relate to their spouse.

Children learn what is honest and true, what has value, and what is to be achieved in one's lifetime from their parents. As a child becomes an adult, most of these values are used as foundations upon which individual personalities are formed and developed. If any of these values need to be restructured, the person must desire it and make the effort to change. It is important in the process of maturing to discover the underlying causes of behaviors, and work to modify dysfunctional ones.

Much can be learned about a future spouse by becoming acquainted with their family and viewing the interaction of the parents. The manner in which a father treats his wife is often an indication of how the son will relate to his new wife. He is also likely to expect to be treated as his mother treats his father. The newlyweds' children will often be raised as each parent was reared by their parents.

The better one knows the inner workings of a fiancé's family, the more information you will have as to the behaviors which may need to be modified and the expectations which need to be adjusted in your mutual efforts to establish a harmonious relationship.

Surfacing Emotions

Immediately following the engagement announcement, there is a time of celebration and excitement when the bride and groom-to-be become the center of attention at social gatherings. This period of euphoria is followed by a time to get back to reality.

Some friends or family members believe that by announcing their engagement and making their love public knowledge, the couple are obligated to share intimate details of their relationship. Questions arise about the length of time the two have known one another, how they will support themselves, when they will have children, if they will live together before the marriage, and what their parents are saying about the engagement.

Underlying emotions may begin to surface as a mother frets over losing her son, or a father his little girl. A parent may be concerned that the fiancé's career will turn the couple into vagabonds with numerous relocations. A sibling or close friend may be jealous that it is not she who is engaged.

The wedding itself is a major social event, and it is sometimes used as an outlet for giving expression to long-held feelings. A groom may want his wedding to surpass that of his older brother, or a parent may compensate for the past neglect of his child. All too frequently the joyous wedding occasion is used to display the affluence of the participants.

Mary and Bill had discussed plans for their wedding and marriage prior to their engagement, but the discussions were focused strictly on the likes and dislikes of weddings they had attended. The only comments made were such as Bill preferring a live band to a D.J., and Mary wanting an evening rather than afternoon wedding.

After the engagement, when Mary and Bill began to discuss the specifics of their wedding, the arguments began. Bill wanted to spend considerably more money than Mary's parents could afford, and he expected to have his needs met. Mary knew her meager savings could not possibly subsidize her parents' allotment, and she wanted the money to set up housekeeping and the honeymoon trip.

Bill wanted eight groomsmen and six ushers. He had a list of over 300 family members, friends, and business associates he wished to invite. Mary had kept her list to only 150. He wanted a candlelight ceremony followed by a ride in a white lighted carriage drawn by a white horse, and then a formal dinner at his father's country club. The band he preferred turned out to be a ten piece orchestra.

At the end of each wedding planning discussion, Mary found herself quarrelsome and angry. Few definite decisions were being made and time was running out.

Bill and Mary did reserve their date for an evening ceremony at her church and placed a deposit with the country club. Mary agreed with both of these decisions, although she knew Bill would need to pare his guest list considerably, and it was not possible to order top-of-the-line dinners for their reception. Bill was not convinced that he would settle for less than the best.

Mary had also placed a deposit on her gown. One she knew would not meet with Bill's elaborate expectations. She became fearful of making any other decisions without Bill's input, but dreaded discussing the plans with him even more.

Until the engagement, Mary's relationship with Bill's mother had been very low-key. Mrs. Davis seemed very cool toward her future daughter-in-law, and Mary was convinced that she thought Bill could do better for himself than to take Mary as his wife.

When Mary and Bill visited his parents on one occasion, Mary summoned her courage and opened the wedding plans to discussion. She sought Mrs. Davis as an ally, explaining her situation and her budget for the wedding. She explained that Bill did not seem to comprehend either her own desires for the wedding or the fact that funds were generous, but limited.

Mrs. Davis, as if ignoring Mary's plight, began to reminisce about her eldest son David's wedding. David had married the only daughter of a prominent lawyer three years earlier—a year before Bill and Mary met.

It was, according to Mrs. Davis, a fairy tale wedding. As if the all-day extravaganza was not enough, it was followed by an elaborate Sunday brunch after which the couple departed for an extended honeymoon in Europe.

For the next several hours, the conversation revolved around David and his precious Gloria. Mary began to realize that every time she and Bill were with his parents, his mother gave a detailed report of David's successes.

It was not that Mary was blind to the sibling rivalry in the Davis' household. It was just that previously it seemed only mildly petty, and she had never perceived it as being threatening to Bill. Now she was beginning to understand Bill's unreasonable behavior regarding their own wedding.

She realized now that Bill had always been plagued by the rivalry and did his best to compete with his older brother. Fueled by his mother's perception of her two sons, Bill had made many of his life choices according to what he thought would top David's accomplishments.

Mary was furious at the thought of David indirectly dictating her wedding style. She wondered if David's accomplishments would also dictate where she would live, how many children she would have and the activities in which they would be involved, the schools they would attend and who they would marry.

That evening when they were alone, Mary laid her findings before Bill. He was enraged. The discussion became quite heated, and they broke the engagement in a fit of anger.

Mary made several attempts in the following days to contact Bill. She was greeted by Mrs. Davis' coolness and Bill's absence. It took Bill a whole week to finally agree to meet Mary.

Together again, Bill acted as if Mary had thrown a temper tantrum; he had allowed her time to cool off; and they must proceed with wedding plans. Mary would not pretend that their problems did not exist.

She decided to stick to their decision to cancel the wedding. They would lose a very small investment, but Mary determined it was necessary to have time to straighten out their lives prior to marriage.

Today Mary and Bill are still dating, but Mary is facing the future cautiously. Bill has begun to recognize the problems he is creating in his life now, and has moved to an apartment of his own in order to avoid hearing of David's glories every time he returns home.

Emotional challenges often arise during life events such as weddings, when stress, time constraints, and changes in lifestyle are occurring. The engagement can be a time when the individual is ill equipped to mentally face the challenge. At times the best solution is to postpone the wedding until the emotional dilemma is solved.

The engagement period is a very emotional time for all the bride and groom and their parents, siblings, and close friends. Parents must face the final "letting go" as their children establish a new family. Friends must accept a change in the bride or groom's status, which often means less flexibility in their relationship.

The bride and groom contend with their own feelings of joy at their union, experience skepticism at some of the aspects of their new life, and feel some regret if they see leaving their parents as a loss, or if the parents express an attitude of loss.

Dealing with Disapproval

Emotional conflict will also arise when one or more family members or friends believe the couple are not suited for each other. The bride or groom may find themselves constantly defending their relationship, while entertaining some of the doubts others have been expressing.

Cheryl Davis met Rich Adams while working a summer retail job. He was assistant manager for the sporting goods department of a major discount chain. Cheryl was earning spending money for her senior year of college.

Once the couple began dating, they immediately spent every free moment together. By the end of the summer, they announced their engagement and planned to be married six months later on Valentine's Day. Cheryl had decided not to return to college, but rather would continue working to save money for her marriage. She reasoned that she would earn her degree through night classes at the local college.

Cheryl's mother, in particular, was adamantly opposed to the marriage. She tried to describe the shortcomings of the relationship to Cheryl from the very beginning. Cheryl ignored her mother, and countless others. Cheryl believed that Rich had proven himself in the business world, because he was already an assistant manager, just three years after completing high school. Cheryl thought her mother was only angry because Cheryl was not returning to school.

When Mrs. Davis mentioned Rich's immaturity, Cheryl said he loved to joke around, just like Cheryl's own father. If Mrs. Davis questioned why they hadn't met Rich's parents, Cheryl just brushed it off as a lack of social training on the part of the Adams. Besides, they were people who liked to keep to themselves. Cheryl almost never saw them.

Mrs. Davis also believed that Cheryl was caught up in a fairy tale. She thought Cheryl was avoiding responsibility by quitting college; looking for a knight to care for her; putting all her energy into a Valentine extravaganza of a wedding; and ignoring Rich's lack of maturity and his strange family life.

There were others who commented to Cheryl about the haste with which she was being married. While not speaking as poignantly as Mrs. Davis, several of Cheryl's friends tried to dissuade Cheryl from what they saw as a disaster. Cheryl thought they were jealous.

At the beginning of the new year, Cheryl started to drop her defenses and listen to the opposition. She began to question herself, but was too caught up in the wedding plans to really pay heed to her own doubts.

Cheryl and Rich were married on Valentine's Day at a "dream-come-true" wedding. In March, Rich was relocated to another state, and Cheryl was forced to find another clerical job. In April, Rich quit his position and spent his days in front of the television set, while Cheryl struggled to support the two of them on her meager salary. When Cheryl tried to make friends in the new area, Rich said he liked to keep to himself.

When she asked about his finding another job, he told her he checked the newspapers regularly.

Eight months after her glorious wedding, Cheryl returned to the Davis residence to get her life in order.

Friends or family are not always correct, and there are times when their doubts for the success of the marriage are based on prejudice, jealousy, or their own sense of loss. It is wise to listen to objections to the marriage and then analyze your own position. If you know your fiancé well, understand your reasons for wanting to spend the rest of your lives together, have reasonable expectations for your relationship and have confidence that the two of you can make the marriage work, then proceed with confidence and commitment and accept their observations as well-intentioned, but mistaken.

Mrs. Eagerman was furious. Her son, Bruce, was returning from the Peace Corp with an Asian bride. Bruce and Chan had been married at a simple civil ceremony in order that Chan could return with Bruce to the United States. They intended to have a private ceremony with the rabbi and then be joined by all Bruce's family and friends at a reception celebration.

Bruce's mother spoke with him long distance listing the numerous reasons why his plan would fail. She was sure that there were too many differences involved in this union to allow for any success. She named cultural, racial, religious, national, and economical differences as tops on her list.

Bruce admitted to his mother that he had entertained all of her objections prior to making the commitment to Chan. Chan, too, had some doubts of her own, but she and Bruce believed they could make their new life work.

When Bruce and Chan arrived in the United States, they rented a small apartment in the city and began seeking employment. Bruce spent his free time arranging for his family and friends to meet Chan in order that they could become acquainted with her and that she could ease into American society.

Chan was able to complete her testing and secure a job as a nurse. She made friends of her own among the nurses at her hospital. Within the safety of that group, Chan was able to receive answers about the behavior of men and women in the United States. The interaction with the patients and her friends also aided the development of her English.

Mrs. Eagerman, while hesitant to accept her son's marriage, could not deny a liking for Chan. As time went on, Bruce's mother found that Chan was not rigid in her Eastern beliefs, and was very anxious to embrace Bruce's way of life. Apparently, Chan had been somewhat of a misfit in her own country, because her beliefs had always leaned to the West. Chan claimed that was her first attraction to Bruce. In Bruce, she had found someone with whom she could identify and feel comfortable.

Blending Values

No matter what the backgrounds of the bride and groom and however similar they may appear on the surface, marriage results in the blending of traditions, values, and beliefs from two different families. The differences may not always be apparent to the couple at first, but they do exist.

If the couple set up a good exchange of their ideas, beliefs, expectations, dreams and goals, they will have a better understanding of their similarities and differences. They must work on the differences to find common ground or acceptance of each other's life styles.

Sarah and Chuck grew up in a little town; they attended the same schools, belonged to the same church, and their parents were members of the same service organization. Upon high school graduation, they obtained employment at the same plant.

When the guest list was compiled for their wedding, the list from the bride's family and the one from the groom's looked almost like carbon copies of each other. Everyone believed this was a match made in heaven.

But the arguments began almost immediately after the wedding. Sarah had the wedding gift money spent before the envelopes were open, while Chuck was mentally depositing it in their account. Chuck's family had always saved for the items they wished to purchase. There were times the children went without new clothes for special occasions. The car often got pretty junky before they bought a new one, but they made purchases when they had the cash to do so.

Sarah had noticed that her family appeared better off than Chuck's family, but she reasoned that her father's income exceeded that of her father-in-law. Sarah had seen her parents use their credit cards or obtain bank loans whenever they wished to make a purchase. She didn't give the matter a second thought, but she did plan to continue the lifestyle to which she was accustomed.

The couple are struggling to find a mutually acceptable financial position. Chuck needs the security of a savings account and minimal debts, and Sarah requires the luxury of material possessions. The two have discovered they must negotiate finances regularly. While every attempt is made to communicate rationally and logically about finances, Sarah and Chuck engage in heated arguments about money nevertheless.

Finances can be a major area of strife within a marriage as Sarah and Chuck discovered. Both individuals had observed their parents' financial styles and had come to believe each method was the right one.

There are a number of facets of each individual's personality which influence the couple's financial picture. One aspect is what money represents to each. Those for whom money symbolizes freedom will behave differently with the family finances than one who sees money as security. The latter will attempt to horde as the former spends freely. Then there are those whose spending and saving habits fluctuate with their mood swings.

It is important to know as much as possible about a future spouse before the marriage, and this is especially true in the area of finances. One indication of your future mate's spending and saving style is to observe and ask questions about his parents' opinions and their methods for dealing with finances. Financial habits an individual has learned in childhood often are brought to the marriage unless a conscious effort is made to change.

Explore the meaning of money as well. The person who interprets money as a source of freedom may ignore the security of tomorrow and live for today. A person who views money as security will seek the stability of a regular salary and job security. This person may sacrifice a career change, even a desirable one, for the security of the known. When money is symbolic of power, a person may become a workaholic, thriving on competition. Objects may be purchased primarily to indicate an achievement of status. A nurturer can be overgenerous with the family funds in order to aid other family members or friends.

The more compatible the styles of the bride and groom, the more smoothly they will be able to determine the spending and saving style of their new union. Change may be necessary on the part of one or both of the partners when the styles are unacceptable or incompatible.

It may be beneficial to determine which person is most comfortable when financial decisions and transactions are to be made, and allow that partner to take the lead during financial discussions. When both have equal experience, the best result may be to divide financial chores. The end result is more important than analyzing how it is to be achieved.

As financial methods can complicate a marriage, families' communication styles are also an area of potential strife for many newlyweds. Each learned how to interact in one way or another with other family members throughout their childhood and young adult years. The lessons of those years will be brought to their marriages.

It is instructive to note the interaction between a partner and his or her parents prior to marriage.

That pattern will soon engulf the new husband or wife.

Martha's family members never raised their voices, not for any reason. If a discussion became heated to the point where someone might be tempted to speak loudly, the matter was dropped and left unresolved. Case closed. The discussion would end and the participants disperse.

In Ron's family, no business was left unfinished. Individuals would shout and gesture wildly until their position was accepted or at least understood. Should one family member choose to end such a heated debate by leaving the room, that was considered a personal attack, a declaration of war!

With the advantage of knowing their two styles of communication, it is relatively easy to predict the disharmony Ron and Martha will experience every time they have opposing opinions. The couple, however, spent many unhappy days arguing, then avoiding each other, and suppressing the issue throughout their engagement and the early years of their marriage. This cycle of tension continued until the two were able to come to grips with their different communication styles.

All learning and growth within a marriage begin with communication, yet if the couple are unable to share their thoughts, development of a successful relationship is obstructed. Marriage requires a secure environment where each individual can share their thoughts, trusting the other to listen without judgment.

Having the freedom to express one's beliefs, values, expectations, and dreams opens the avenue for discussion. Through discussion, the couple can find mutual ground from which to build their marriage.

Many couples discover long before their wedding vows that marriage is more than the union of two individuals. Unless the couple is totally isolated from and have no communication with their parents, there will be a need to incorporate the parents into the new family unit.

Marriage is one of the few areas of a person's life where a long-time commitment is made to total strangers. When a man or woman promises to marry, there is an implied pledge to regard the family of their intended as their own.

There are families that have very specific and rigid ideas about how holidays, birthdays, and special occasions are to be celebrated. Some parental dictates even extend into the area of vacations.

It is wise to discuss in advance of the wedding how much time will be spent with the extended family. It is also helpful to determine how much flexibility there will be to alter arrangements over the years. It may be easy to spend a particular holiday or occasion with both families until children are born. Children will limit the amount of time that can be spent away from home if only because of the children's schedules.

What to Call In-laws

Another issue which arises regarding in-laws is the question of how they are to be addressed. This issue is best faced early on so as to avoid potentially awkward situations. Some newlyweds attempt to ignore the perplexity, and they avoid addressing in-laws at all. This becomes impossible over the telephone or when calling across a crowded room.

The names chosen need to indicate a respect for the parents, while taking into account the personalities and ages of those involved. A spouse who is close in age to his in-laws will find Mom and Dad as inappropriate as Mr. and Mrs. In this case, first names may work best.

While socially correct, using Mom and Dad to address one's in-laws may not be comfortable to the newlywed, because the names are reserved for one's own parents.

Another alternative is to use Mother Smith or Mother Betty to address a mother-in-law. This indicates both respect and familiarity.

Whatever name is chosen to address in-laws, it is best to discuss the choice with the parents in case they have objections or preferences. Even the original name chosen may change over time, such as when Mom gives way to Grandma.

A Changing Phase

Marriage, family, and life itself are all about change. Just as one name gives way to another, each phase of life makes way for the new. Each stage of development is experienced more effectively by the couple who have worked to nurture their compatibility and open the channels of communication.

The course can be set for a successful marriage as the bride and groom interact between themselves and with their families during the engagement, each individual making a conscious effort to modify their own rules for living to be consistent with those of their partner.

The process of incorporating the two original families into the newly formed family begins with the engagement and continues over time as all family members mature, relationships change, and additions occur to the family. In the meantime, decisions must be made for the wedding day.

3

From Dream Wedding to Reality

A great many decisions must be made in the process of planning a wedding. As preparations proceed, not only do the bride and groom need to agree about plans, but family members may also have to consent.

Initial decisions which must be made include date and location, time of day, size, budget, and who will pay for the wedding. The answers to these questions will have a bearing on the remaining choices.

For example, the location of the wedding may determine the number of guests who are able to attend, and the number of guests dictates the reception facility choices. The parties funding the wedding will establish the size of the budget and this will affect virtually all of the other decisions.

Visualize Your Wedding

The bride can form her initial plans by creating an image of her dream wedding. What mood and tempo are desired? Soft candlelight and romance, with a very couple-centered wedding or a joyous, jubilant, festive celebration embracing large numbers of family and friends? To serve everyone's taste, the ceremony could focus on the couple, the dinner could emphasize the family, and the reception could concentrate on everyone.

Think of the setting where the wedding will occur. Will the ceremony be conducted in a place of worship, or do other locations appeal? Some options to explore include a garden, historical site, a room at a banquet facility, someone's home, a boat, or the courthouse.

Consider the bride's appearance. Is the look to be formal or casual? Will the gown be sophisticated, glamorous, romantic, simple, or cute? How will the bridesmaids' gowns blend with the bride's? What color or colors will they wear? What mood will the colors project?

At the early stages of the planning process, the bride can create a vision of her dream wedding without limitations. She can let her imagination run free in order to determine the most appealing type of wedding.

Susan was anchored to the telecast of Prince Charles and Lady Di's wedding, absorbed in every detail of the event. Naturally, when it came time to plan her wedding, she had envisioned much of her dream wedding.

Knowing her vision of an ideal wedding was not Susan's problem. Her problem was making it a reality. Susan and Tom agreed to split the cost of the wedding with Susan's parents, but even with four persons contributing to the event, funds were still limited.

By deciding exactly what was essential to her, Susan was able to concentrate her attention on identifying options which met her criteria and fit her mother's budget. Where cost was an inhibiting factor, Susan borrowed, purchased used items, or negotiated. Susan had her ideal gown sewn for her. Costs were trimmed by using less expensive fabrics. Susan used the same method for the bridesmaids' dresses.

The guest list, kept to only 100 persons, saved on expenses. The horse and carriage, though an extravagance, was a must for Susan. She justified the extra cost of the carriage for her and Tom by borrowing cars for the attendants.

Within reason, Susan did accomplish her ideal wedding. Much of the credit for her success can be attributed to knowing what she wanted.

The first vision the bride creates need not be the one on which she acts. Initial thoughts may prove impractical once the planning has begun, and the bride has received the input from wedding supply experts.

Clara was certain she did not want a wedding like any other she had attended. She decided on an afternoon affair at a banquet facility. The ceremony would occur in one room, and the guests would move to another for champagne and hors d'oeuvres. An orchestra would entertain.

Clara envisioned herself in a brocade suit. She would have no wedding cake, and she would not toss her bouquet.

As she began to gather pricing and talk with suppliers, Clara found that a traditional wedding gown was more readily available, and therefore more reasonably priced. The champagne and hors d'oeuvres were almost as costly as providing a meal for her guests, and the wedding cake would be included in the dinner price quoted by the banquet hall.

The majority of her guests would prefer to dance to a rock band than listen to an orchestra.

Slowly Clara's original vision began to change. She pictured herself in a sophisticated wedding gown, dancing to a large band, after having enjoyed a dinner at the banquet facility.

Once the bride has established her own dream, it is time to determine how her vision conflicts or is in accord with the groom's concept. The bride can ask him the same questions she has asked herself. At what location does he see himself being married. Who are the people around him. What time of day is it. How formal is the occasion.

Very often the bride-to-be will discover that her fiancé has not spent much time thinking about the entire wedding, but wants certain aspects done one particular way.

Roger expressed a very definite desire to include his two brothers and his eight college buddies in the wedding party. Karen was initially at a loss as to how she would cope with Roger's preference. It seemed to Karen that she had the freedom to plan the wedding to her specifications, with the exception of the wedding party.

Karen didn't know ten women capable and willing to invest the amount of money it would take to be in her bridal party, and she didn't want that many persons at the altar with her and Roger.

After much deliberation, Roger agreed that Karen should ask those women she really wanted to be bridesmaids, and he would match groomsmen to them. The additional men would be ushers.

A different situation arose for Ann when she made appointments to talk with photographers and videographers. Steven, an amateur photographer, understood many of the technical aspects of the art and had some very stringent requirements. Ann became so tired of listening to Steven badger the photographers and videographers they interviewed, that she told Steven to find the technicians he approved, and she would abide by his decision.

It is necessary to take the two visions and merge them into one custom-made wedding. The bride and groom will both have had the opportunity to give input into the creation of their special day. With that mission accomplished, it is time for reality to seep in. Ideas must be modified to some extent to accommodate parental wishes, budget, number of guests, climate, and so on. But remember, those desires most important to the couple can be retained.

Parental Participation

The extent to which the parents of the bride and groom participate in the plans is unique to each couple. Many times, the mother-of-the-bride assumes the traditional role of hostess on the wedding day. The mother of today's bride usually acts as an advisor, and rarely is in charge of the whole affair. More often than in the past, it is the couple who plan and finance their wedding.

The groom's mother may be asked for opinions and offer direction to the couple as well. The fathers rarely get involved in the details of the wedding plans, but may wish to be informed about various decisions.

Hidden Agendas

Any one of the wedding participants may attempt to satisfy their hidden agenda. These generally are agendas which cause the person to make a particular decision or take action primarily to fulfill an emotional need of which one may not be consciously aware.

A father may borrow funds to give his "little girl" the best of everything for her wedding because he feels guilty about not meeting all her emotional needs as she was growing up.

A father-in-law may offer to contribute to the wedding costs because he's afraid the bride's family will not do a decent job on their own. He doesn't want to be embarrassed in front of his business associates.

A mother-of-the-bride may try to have the wedding she never had through her daughter. And a bride may be trying to show her college friends that she has achieved a social rank.

Whatever the motivation behind the actions, any of these hidden agendas can result in conflict during the planning stages. Being aware that they exist is a step toward recognition of any sensitive areas which may arise. Once recognized, they can be discussed.

Who Pays

One area that can control the outcome of the wedding more than any other is budget. The size of the guest list, the formality of the occasion, the number of attendants, the amount and quality of entertainment, the choice of floral arrangements, and the bridal attire are just some of the factors affecting the cost of a wedding.

Once Susan began making arrangements for her wedding, she found her plans strongly conflicted with those of her mother. At each level of planning, Susan and Paul would discuss their desires, determine how they budget the wedding, and then Susan would take the thoughts to her mother for validation.

Even though the couple were financing the wedding, Susan's mom vetoed every idea without fail. Susan and Paul wanted a small garden wedding, with the ceremony in a gazebo, and the reception under a tent. Her mother would attend nothing less than a church wedding.

Susan had chosen black and white for the attendants of both the bride and groom. Susan's mother could not envision bridesmaids in black, even though Susan produced evidence of the color's popularity.

The idea of a buffet meal, which allowed guests to wander and mingle, appealed to Susan and Paul, while the bride's mother wanted to serve plate dinners.

Susan and Paul had no prior experience planning a social event, but they did their homework. They worked within their budget to create the atmosphere desired. Susan began to realize that the only mistake in the plans was that she looked to her mother for approval.

Susan's parents had just celebrated their 35th wedding anniversary, and Susan was their only daughter. There was no reason Susan's mother should be aware of current wedding trends. Once Susan realized the situation and accepted the fact that she had financial control, she stopped seeking her mother's approval, and attempted to educate her mother about modern weddings. Susan still sought her mother's advice regarding social customs, but persuaded her mother to accept, or at least tolerate, the couple's wedding plans.

The balance of the wedding was planned with less stress and greater progress. Susan and Paul were both capable of deciding what it was they wanted, and they found a way to make their plans happen.

Many couples are financing their weddings, as Susan and Paul chose to do, but that was not always the practice. Historically, there was a need for families to have their daughters marry men who were able to support them. This necessity required the father of the bride to offer the best terms and incur the entire cost of the marriage ceremony and celebration.

As time progressed and customs and values changed, the groom and his family began to assume a small portion of the expenditures. Then came what we consider today to be the traditional division of expenses:

Bridegroom's financial responsibilities
Engagement and bride's wedding ring
Marriage license
Bridal bouquet
Flowers for both mothers
Corsage for honored female guests (grandmothers, godmothers, special aunt, and so on..)
Gift for the bride
Boutonnieres for groomsmen
Officiant's fee
Honeymoon
Housing for his out-of-town guests
Presents for his attendants

Bride's financial responsibilities
Groom's wedding ring
Gift for the groom
Hair and beauty expenses
Gifts for her attendants
Her medical examination
Bridesmaid's luncheon
Housing for her out-of-town guests
Stationery for personal notes and thank yous
Wedding guest book

Expenses incurred by groom's family
Their travel and housing
Their clothes
Wedding gift for the couple
Rehearsal dinner

Expenses incurred by bride's family

The balance of the expenses, such as:

Bridal attire and trousseau

Invitations and announcements

Floral arrangements and bouquets

Boutonniere for bride's father

Corsages for special friends

Rental of ceremony site

Music for ceremony

Bridal consultant

Transportation

Entire cost of reception

Other miscellaneous expenses

As costs began to escalate, it became common practice for the groom's family to pick up the bar tab from the reception. By paying the beverage bill, the groom's family was able to decrease the large expenditure assumed by the family of the bride.

Today, there are no fixed rules about the division of expenses. When the family of the bride is incapable of assuming the financial burden of a wedding, the couple have been known to pay for the entire event. The couple may also pay for their wedding when the bride is marrying for the second time. If the groom's family has more wealth than the bride's, they may choose to pay for the reception as a gift to the couple. When the bride's family is traditional in their values, they may insist on organizing and financing the ceremony and reception.

Controlling Decisions

One reason that a couple may assume the entire cost of their wedding is to have control of its planning. Couples who marry later in life have already established themselves to some extent financially. They most likely wish to choose their own style for celebrating their marriage, and they know by holding the purse strings they have the power of choice.

Nadine and Philip met at a financial planning seminar. She is a lawyer, and he is in real estate. After a short period of time, they found themselves agreeing to what was totally out-of-the-question a short time before. They were engaged to be married.

Nadine could not imagine herself as the traditional bride, and Philip was content to follow her wishes. She planned a small ceremony in St. Thomas. Their closest family members and friends were invited to attend the ceremony and were given air tickets to the island.

A tropical celebration was planned at a local lounge the weekend following the nuptials. Two hundred guests were invited to the reception to celebrate with Nadine and Philip.

This was not the wedding Nadine's parents would have planned for their daughter. While they did not totally approve of the event, the decisions were not theirs to make.

When a gift is given, it is to be given unconditionally. That is the nature of a gift. Unfortunately, when it comes to giving the couple a wedding, there are frequently strings attached.

Some parents believe they need to get a fair exchange for their money. Since the mother-of-the-bride is the traditional hostess of the event, parents believe they should have some degree of control of the plans for the wedding.

Diane had been away at college for four years and now lived in an apartment down the street from her parents. As soon as Diane announced her engagement to Mike, her parents began to take control of the planning.

They didn't like the date the couple had chosen. It was too close to Christmas, and their family wouldn't travel over Christmas. The engagement ring was too modern; it looked like a cocktail ring. Why didn't they plan to start their married life in Diane's apartment and save some money? The list of objections and directions went on.

When Diane was informed that money had been placed in an account to cover the entire cost of her wedding, she was thrilled. She had been concerned that she and Mike would need to contribute to their wedding. Money was tight for them now as they were just beginning their careers, so her parents' news gave her relief, initially.

As plans progressed, Diane found she had little to no say in organizing her wedding. The date was moved to February. The restaurant was her parents' favorite. The church was, of course, the one attended by her family. The music was to be provided by a friend of her father's.

Diane was allowed to choose her wedding gown, but only under the close supervision of her mother. She began to realize that all she and Mike needed to do was show up on the date dictated by her parents.

While being thoughtless, Diane's parents had no intention of being cruel. They were merely falling into the parent/child role they had assumed all of Diane's life. They chose her activities and paid for them. They chose her college and paid for it. They had even discouraged Diane's working part-time at any point of her life in order that she would have more time for her studies. Whenever she required money, they provided it, as long as she would abide by their wishes.

Mike and Diane released the privilege to plan their wedding by surrendering financial control to Diane's parents. This pattern he couple are willing to accept financial support from the parents.

The groom's family is often ignored when wedding plans are made. His family does have the right to invite guests, but otherwise have little influence over the wedding plans. The parents of the groom are treated as invited guests, just like all the others on the guest list.

With the traditional division of expenses no longer intact, the groom's parents may buy an interest in the wedding plans by offering to pay a portion of the total expense or choose certain areas to finance.

Jack's father, George Williams plays with the local symphony. He also substitutes for a number of the major local theaters. Mr. Williams loves music and knows exactly what to expect from any artist.

When Jack and Marilyn were planning their wedding, Mr. Williams was concerned about the vocalists and musicians at the ceremony. He believed there should be chamber music during dinner and big band sounds for dancing at the reception.

Marilyn was leaning toward the church organist and a small band to play after dinner. Realizing that he would not get the quality he wanted for his quests, Mr. Williams interceded. He requested the opportunity to plan and purchase the musical aspects of the wedding. Jack and Marilyn gladly left the music in his capable hands.

The parents of the groom may certainly request a more active role in plans if it is their desire. They may feel more comfortable doing so by making a contribution to the overall expense of the day.

When Rick and Marge were planning their wedding, Rick's parents realized how one-sided the guest list appeared. Marge's family was spread across the country, while most of Rick's family were right in their hometown. Rick's guests outnumbered Marge's five to one. Rick's parents were uncomfortable having Marge's family pay for so many of their guests and graciously offered to split the cost of the reception.

With all six persons having a financial stake in the wedding, the planning sessions became social events for all three couples, as they regularly gathered for dinner to discuss ideas.

Making decisions by dollars is not always as clear cut as it was with Marilyn's wedding or as warm and loving as it was with Marge's. Often the parent or the couple do not even realize that they are purchasing their right to decide how the wedding is to be organized. There is only a feeling that they should be getting something in return for their expenditure. By being aware of this power, a couple can avoid some hazards and make it work for rather than against them.

Compromising

Compromising portions of the wedding plans may require different persons to agree on decisions. The bride may need to compromise with her bridesmaids regarding the wedding day gowns. In the past, the bride was able to select the style and color, but current prices make most brides hesitant to demand their own choices.

The wedding date may need to reflect convenience for the guests. If a large number of those invited are in college, the wedding date may be determined by a school break.

The type of music chosen may be governed by the desires of those guests most likely to dance.

Negotiation skills become an asset when there is such a diversity of people and so many aspects of the wedding day to be planned and orchestrated.

Being certain of what one wants, the availability and cost, and having a budget with which to work is half the battle. The rest is knowing how many persons are involved in the decision making process and how agreements can best be reached.

4

Who Will Attend

A major event often develops as a reflection of the personalities and number of persons involved. A necessary stage in the wedding planning process is to determine who will attend. Decisions regarding the number of bridesmaids, groomsmen, and guests must be made before the wedding facility can be selected. Knowing specifically who those persons are may also affect decisions regarding location, time of the day, formality, menu, and entertainment for the wedding.

Choosing Attendants

A wedding day is the bride and groom's own special moment in time. It is one of the days in their lives when they will play the leading roles and possess center stage.

The supporting cast is comprised of those persons chosen to be bridal attendants and groomsmen. They generally share a special relationship with the bride and groom.

Maryelise asked her fiancé's only sister to be her maid-of-honor. Maryelise and Cathy had grown to be friends, and she now wanted to symbolize their sisterhood at the time of her wedding.

Roberta requested her future stepdaughter to assume the role of maid-of-honor, with the hopes that the position would portray the closeness she felt for the young woman.

Jack had felt particularly close to his father since his mother's death in his early teens. Even though he had left his father's home at the time he entered college, they had retained a special relationship. When it came time to choose his groomsmen, Jack wanted none other than his father for his best man.

Marie and Kim had been best friends throughout their entire life. While they were separated during their high school years, they had remained in touch and had resumed their relationship in college. It was only natural that the two should choose one another for honor attendants at each other's wedding.

While it is important to the well-being of the bride and groom to be surrounded by special people on their wedding day, consideration also needs to be given the tasks those persons are to perform. It is important to select attendants who will serve the bridal couple efficiently and cheerfully.

The honor attendant has the most glamorous role, but the best man is given the most tasks. The best man's duties include:

Arrange for the bachelor party

Coordinate purchase of gift from groomsmen

Be responsible for the bride's ring

Help the groom dress and get to the ceremony

Present the check to the officiant

Sign the marriage license

Drive the newlyweds to the reception (if there is no limousine)

Sit at the bride's right side at the bridal table

Propose the first toast

Read telegrams sent to the bride and groom

Dance with the bride

Dance with the honor attendant

Arrange for the newlyweds' luggage to be accessible

Help the groom prepare to leave the reception

Arrange transportation from the reception

Persons most frequently chosen for the role of best man are the brother of the groom or one of the groom's close friends.

The honor attendant is designated as the maid-of-honor when she is single, and the matron-of-honor when she is married. Should the bride choose to have two honor attendants, a maid and a matron, the maid-of-honor takes precedence, and the matron acts as her assistant. The honor attendant has the following tasks:

Plan the bridal shower

Coordinate the purchase of the bridesmaids' wedding gift

Help the bride dress for the wedding

Be responsible for the groom's ring

Hold the bridal bouquet and adjust the veil and train during the ceremony

Stand at the groom's side in the receiving line

Sign the marriage license

Sit at the groom's left at the bridal table

Dance with the groom

Dance with the best man

Help the bride change to leave the reception

The bride's sister will most often serve as honor attendant. Other choices are a best friend, a close cousin, or the groom's sister, if she is well known to the bride. The bride's mother is the hostess of the event, and therefore should not be requested to serve as honor attendant. The role of hostess takes precedence over that of honor attendant.

Bridesmaids and groomsmen have far fewer duties. All the attendants stand in front of the guests during the ceremony and walk down the aisle. They also assume seats at the bridal table and participate in a dance with one another after the bride and groom's first dance and the newlyweds' dance with their parents.

Additionally, the bridesmaids may be requested to stand in the receiving line, and the groomsmen may be required to serve as ushers before the ceremony if none have been assigned. Two groomsmen are chosen to escort each of the mothers down the aisle before the ceremony.

Inviting Guests

Establishing the guest list is the next important step in preparing for the wedding event. The guests are invited to witness the beginning of the marriage, and then celebrate the event along with the bride and groom.

There are some who will be automatically invited because of their relationship within the family, and others who are invited because of the social relationship they share with one of the parents or the bride and groom.

The guest list will also be affected by a number of outside factors, such as the location of the ceremony and celebration, the size and proximity of the two families, the number of guests the reception facility can accommodate, the formality of the reception, if children are included as guests, and the amount of money available to pay for the reception.

The bride's parents have family members and friends they will wish to invite to the wedding, as will the parents of the groom and the bride and groom.

One common method for creating the guest list is to begin with four separate lists. The two mothers, the bride, and the groom may make separate lists of the persons they wish to appear on the guest list. There will be duplications of names, one of which can be eliminated. The four lists can then be merged into one. This merged list will then need to be pared to match the size of the reception facility and the budget.

The paring of the list can be an emotionally charged experience, and it is best to be prepared to discuss this procedure calmly with those involved.

If both families reside within the same geographic area, and the families are approximately the same size, the total number of guests should be equally divided between the groom's family and the bride's family.

Ann decided to complete her college degree in California after meeting Ralph during his senior year at Northern Illinois University. His plans were to return to the family business in Los Angeles after his graduation. Ann had two years of college to complete.

During their two years in California together, Ann and Ralph allowed their relationship to grow. They became engaged and decided to marry the June after her graduation.

Most of Ralph's friends, many of Ann's, and all of the business relations were in California. Ann had family scattered across the United States, but the majority of them were in Illinois. The couple discussed the pros and cons of being married in one state and then the other. They decided to be married in California.

Their decision greatly affected the balance of the guest list. When the list was completed, Ralph's side of the list outnumbered Ann's ten to one.

Ralph and Ann also decided not to burden Ann's parents with more than the expenses for their attire and their travel. Ralph and Ann planned to finance the wedding themselves, but were later assisted by Ralph's family.

There are times when parents want a person or a family included on their list that the bride or groom does not. This was the circumstance for Maryann. All of her life Maryann hid from her mother's cousin, Ruth, at family gatherings. Ruth was selfish and nasty, and she particularly liked to single Maryann out and berate her. Ruth thought Maryann was too fat, and too lazy.

Years later Maryann had become an attractive woman and found her place in the business world, but she still avoided Ruth. She declined invitations to family gatherings which included Ruth, and she avoided visiting her mother when she knew Ruth might be there.

When Maryann saw Ruth's name on the guest list for her wedding she was outraged. They had agreed to invite only her parents' siblings and to not extend the list to include their cousins.

Maryann's mother contended that while Ruth was disagreeable, she was a close relative. Maryann said she should not be subjected to anyone's rudeness at her own wedding.

The battle went on for quite some time without resolution. Maryann's mother was the hostess for the wedding, and officially she would be extending the invitations.

It wasn't until Maryann threatened to elope that her mother began to listen to her pleas. For a number of years, Maryann had not been present at any other event to which Ruth was invited, so why should Maryann be forced to be with Ruth at her own wedding.

Maryann's mother extended a personal phone call to Ruth. She explained that Maryann had limited the guest list to only immediate family because of the limited space at the banquet hall. In fairness to everyone, they were making no exceptions.

Of course Ruth was furious at Maryann and her mother. Maryann's mother felt bad about the situation also, but she knew it was impossible to please everyone. When it came to her daughter's wedding, she decided to please the bride.

Children: Yes or No

The situation becomes even more emotional when the issue turns to children and the guest list. A decision needs to be made regarding children as guests prior to compiling the invitation list.

If children are omitted, the invitations are addressed to Mr. and Mrs., and the inside envelope shows the first names of the parents only. This is a clear indication to the addressee that children are not included.

Should children be invited as guests, their names are written on the inner envelope. Children thirteen years old or older may receive their own invitation, but it is appropriate to include them with their parents until age eighteen.

Because of the cost of a wedding reception, there may be a desire to limit the guest list to adults. If this is the case, the information should be spread among family members and friends prior to mailing the invitations. This way, no one will be caught by surprise.

If there are known persons who are sensitive to the issue and may pose a problem or create an argument once the invitation is received, it is wise for the mother of the bride or groom to phone them and discuss the situation prior to mailing the invitations. It may be calmly explained that children will not be included. It is appropriate to state that the late hours are not good for children, and the cost prohibits their inclusion.

When children are omitted from the guest list, invitations are mailed to Mr. and Mrs., indicating that only the adults are to be present at the wedding. In spite of this, however, requests for exceptions are to be expected. The couple need to anticipate this in advance and agree on the appropriate degree of rigidity.

Catherine received a phone call from one of her close friends shortly after mailing the invitations to her wedding. Her friend had a four-month old baby who was nursing, and she requested permission to bring her baby to Catherine's wedding.

Trina's mother received a request from a business associate. The associate's husband would be out-of-town; could she bring her ten-year-old daughter in his place.

Maureen received a letter from her fiancé's out-of-state aunt. They were bringing their four children to the area for the weekend. There was no one to care for the children while they were at the wedding; could they bring the children along?

Kristi received a response card indicating five persons were attending the wedding when only two adults were invited.

Some or all of these situations occur when planning a wedding, and it is very difficult to make an exception for one guest and not for others. The bride and her family need to decide on the position which they believe is most fair to everyone and then be firm to that position.

At times it is necessary to call the invitee and explain that the response card was incorrect. A gracious explanation of why children are being omitted is in order.

As an option, the bride's family may hire a responsible caretaker for the children of guests.

Guests also need to be made aware when their requests are placing the bride or her family in a very awkward situation. Often, unless informed by the bride's family, the guest believes she is the only one with a particular request.

There is one school of thought which says that weddings are for adults. Children waste food, monopolize the dance floor, and become too tired to be civilized.

This is not to suggest that children should always be omitted from the wedding activities. A wedding is an important life event, and one from which children need not be excluded.

Linda and Ron both love children. They plan to have several of their own to add to the two they already have from Linda's first marriage. When it came time to make the guest list, they could not dream of excluding the cousins and friends of Linda's children. Nor could they omit Ron's many nieces and nephews.

The guest list began to look like a school roster, but Linda and Ron were pleased with their choices. Because so many children were involved, they decided to host their reception at the local park district building. The building was quite nice. It had adequate restrooms and a kitchen. The banquet room was nicely decorated, and the numerous picture windows overlooked a grassy vista.

The building had the perfect atmosphere for adults to visit with one another during dinner, and for children to go out and run after dinner.

Because the facilities were so lovely, and the location so ideal, Linda and Ron also decided to have a very brief ceremony in the park setting, with the reception immediately following.

Ann and Ted wanted to have their many nieces and nephews included in their special day. They planned their wedding events, thinking of the children as much as the adults.

There would be approximately one hour between the end of the ceremony and the beginning of cocktail service at the reception. Dinner was not to be served until 7:00 P.M. Ann knew that her sister's five children were accustomed to having dinner at 5:00 P.M. She was equally sure that other children did not often wait until 7:00 P.M. for dinner.

Ann spoke with the church hostess about the possibility of having finger food and punch in the church basement after the ceremony. Because of her thoughtful planning, the guests were provided a location to eat and mingle while the bride and groom posed for the photographer. Additionally, there were numerous happy children in attendance at the wedding.

It is also necessary to be aware of children's feelings and endurance levels when including them in the bridal party. If a child is terrified of walking down the aisle, or even a little shy, take the pressure off everyone. Let whatever happens be all right. Know that the main purpose has been served merely by including the child in the special day. It is always possible to have the photographs as a recollection, even if the child never makes it to the front of the aisle.

Accommodating Guests

Other factors will influence the decisions a bride and groom or their parents may make during the planning stages of their wedding. Just as Linda and Ron planned their wedding to accommodate children, many couples make other decisions regarding their ceremonies and receptions to have the day go as smoothly as possible.

In some cases, the location and the date of a ceremony are determined by the requirements of the religious officiant.

If an outdoor ceremony is desired, the date must be determined by the climate. The best outdoor location is an area that provides access to the indoors should the weather be unfavorable.

The number of persons a facility can accommodate is another consideration before reserving a building for the ceremony. There is a need to calculate the number of guests who will be capable of accepting the invitation to the reception and witnessing the ceremony. It's wise to take into account the guest's schedules before setting the wedding date. If most of the guests must travel to the wedding, plan a time when they are more likely to have the freedom to do so, such as when the weather is mild, and children are on vacation from school.

If a wedding is to be scheduled close to a major holiday, consider the plans most guests may have made for other activities. Friday evening weddings are becoming more common, but guests must have time to prepare for the ceremony after returning from the day's work. Sunday weddings must take into account the early schedule many workers and students have on Monday morning.

The better the wedding schedule is arranged to meet the needs of the bridal families, as well as the guests, the happier everyone will be.

The location and time of the wedding reception is most often determined by that of the ceremony. Many brides try to schedule just enough time for photographs between the ceremony and reception.

Should there be a large amount of time between the two events, the mother-of-the bride often invites guests to her home for refreshments and to view the wedding gifts already received. While this aspect of the wedding day is pleasant, it places another burden on the family.

Jennifer and John live in a suburban area of Chicago. They planned their twelve o'clock noon ceremony at a Roman Catholic cathedral in the city, just north of the downtown. One of the priests at the church is Jennifer's uncle, who will officiate at the wedding ceremony.

Plans have also been made to have a formal dinner reception at one of the grand old hotels in the heart of the downtown. The dinner will be at seven o'clock that evening, with cocktails being served one hour prior.

The schedule allows Jennifer and John to have photographs and video taken at a number of beautiful spots in the city. In addition to the time they will spend in the cathedral, they will be filmed along Chicago's lakefront, at the beautiful rose gardens near by, and Buckingham Fountain. To capture these shots, the limo and the photographer and videographer must drive and park a few times. The five hours will go quickly for the bridal couple.

The guests, however, need to be entertained during that large block of time. They will have driven approximately 30 miles to the ceremony, and are unlikely to return home before the reception. The city offers numerous activities, but these guests will be dressed for a formal dinner at a lovely hotel.

It was important to the bride to have her guests witness the wedding ceremony, but it became apparent that most guests would forego the ceremony and only attend the reception if Jennifer did not make arrangements for the time between the two events.

During the search for a solution, a small family deli was discovered near the cathedral. The owners of the restaurant had decorated a back room for banquet purposes. The food was fresh and tasty, and the facilities were clean and adequate for Jennifer's purposes. She would have liked to serve luncheon at the hotel, but this restaurant met her budget requirements.

Jennifer reserved the space for her guests. After seeing the bridal couple drive off toward the lakefront, Jennifer's guests would walk to the restaurant for petite sandwiches and punch. They would be allowed to sit and converse until four o'clock.

Once they had completed their luncheon, they would drive and park in the garage near the hotel. From that location it would be possible to walk to the lake for the scenic view and back to the hotel in time for cocktails. Jennifer had fulfilled her obligation to consider her guests' comfort.

The number of guests and the times and locations of the ceremony and reception are the first indications of the mood the guests will experience during the wedding celebration. Jennifer planned a wedding that moved from formal in the cathedral, to casual at the deli, and back to formal at the hotel reception.

Guests appreciate knowing the formality of attire they are expected to wear to the wedding, and the invitation is the guest's first indication of the wedding's style. Formal invitations are very plain white or ivory with traditional wording engraved or thermographed on the stationery, while casual invitations are available in a variety of colors and styles. Invitation catalogs are divided into sections according to the level of formality the bride and groom wish to achieve.

The bride and groom, along with their families, create the atmosphere they most enjoy for the celebration of a lifetime.

After decisions regarding style, formality, and size of the wedding have been made, the next step is to find those persons who can best supply the goods and services required for the wedding.

5
Selecting
Suppliers

Finding and working with wedding suppliers can be daunting when faced with all the other tasks which must be accomplished before the wedding. There are, however, ways to make the process easier and more enjoyable. Three key skills which must be developed to facilitate this process are communication, creativity, and contract know-how. All these can be acquired with a minimum of effort. First, as much information as possible must be accumulated.

How to Find

Inform yourself by reading about wedding planning, talking with newlyweds, assisting friends with their wedding plans, asking parents their opinions about wedding suppliers, and then searching out and interviewing the various suppliers.

Most parents have experience planning social events, and their knowledge is helpful to the wedding couple. They may have information regarding the reputations of various suppliers, know-how to negotiate for services, and have developed basic planning skills.

Toni and Ed were determined to have the wedding

of their dreams, and they resolved to plan it their way, on their budget. They were headstrong about their decisions, wanting no outside interference from anyone.

The couple considered a local caterer with an excellent reputation, but friends had warned that the prices were high. Consequently, Toni and Ed decided on an inexpensive choice, without comparison shopping.

Toni's father had information which would have helped the couple had they asked for his opinion. He had attended his company's Christmas party only a month earlier, catered by the local caterer. At the party, he learned the caterer had just opened a banquet facility, and was offering special pricing as an incentive for couples to use the facility. Had they availed themselves of this information, they could have gone with their original inclination.

Parents have often attended social functions, talked with parents of other newlyweds, or planned their own events. They have the knowledge couples may need to get their wedding plans off to a successful start.

Another method for gaining first-hand information is to assist with the planning of a friend or relative's wedding.

Nancy was the maid-of-honor at Kate's wedding, just eight months prior to her own wedding date. She assisted Kate with wedding plans by doing the telephone screening of suppliers. All the while, Nancy kept detailed notes for herself, as well as for Kate.

Nancy and Kate visited a number of suppliers, and Nancy checked their references. She was able to observe the end result at Kate's wedding. Nancy took advantage of an excellent opportunity to gain information for her own wedding while helping Kate.

Know-how may also be gained by drawing on the information of knowledgeable persons. Many suppliers belong to a network of wedding suppliers. Once one reputable supplier has been found, that person may offer the names of other suppliers with whom he has worked and been pleased.

Photographers have worked with numerous bands, florists, and others. They have observed their work and how they interacted with the bride and groom. A photographer's opinion may well be worth considering when seeking other suppliers.

Teri decided she wanted to be married in a Renaissance setting. She had a friend who would cater the party with olde English foods, but beyond arranging the meal, Teri had no other resources to call on in making her selections.

The bride-to-be found a bridal consultant listed in her phone directory and called for information. The consultant contacted the local rental shop and a convention site which was once a monastery. The convention facility offered the name of a Justice of the Peace, a minstrel group, and a specialty florist. The consultant observed their services and checked their references. In no time at all, Teri had her Renaissance wedding planned.

A detailed list of wedding suppliers is an essential step to creating the wedding, and there are a number of ways to compile a list.

Friends are a good source of reference for competent suppliers. Ask recently married friends or those who have attended weddings for the names of suppliers. Ask what was memorable about the supplier's services, how the wedding couple was treated, if the price was fair, and if complications arose and how were they handled by the supplier.

Names of the various suppliers are also listed in wedding directories and magazines. Local suppliers are targeted in the Yellow Pages of the phone book and in the special bridal sections produced several times a year by newspapers. Most often these bridal editions occur close to Valentine's Day, in June, and after Christmas. Wedding suppliers advertise their services in these newspapers, and editors often interview selected business owners.

Record Keeping

Initial contact may be made with wedding suppliers via the telephone to determine availability of date, services rendered, and price. Often brochures can be mailed which detail the information offered during the phone conversation and display photographs of the services available. Before completing the phone conversation, be sure to have the name of the person who provided the information and record it for future use.

The phone interviews offer an ideal time to begin the record keeping which will be necessary throughout the planning stages of the wedding. The more accurate the records, the more smoothly tasks will be accomplished.

A separate notebook sheet can be used for each acceptable supplier who is available on the wedding date. Pertinent information, such as the following, can be recorded:

Supplier name:

Address:

Phone number:

Contact person:

Helpfulness and courtesy of

contact person:

Hours of business:

Services available:

Number of weddings they serve per day:

Price:

Booking deadline:

Deposit requirement:

Cancellation policy:

Appointment time and date:

If the supplier warrants further investigation, an appointment can be made during the first phone contact and recorded on the sheet. If there is doubt about some aspect of the service and price, or discomfort experienced due to the contact person's behavior, make a notation of it and wait to weigh the merit of other suppliers before proceeding.

Before Signing the Contract

During the phone interview, or during the first appointment ask about insurance coverage. In the event of an accident, learn how the supplier will remedy the situation. This information is important for the protection of the bride and groom, as well as their guests. The information should be recorded in the contract. As with any contract, all agreements and understandings should be in writing to prevent unpleasant surprises on the wedding day.

The telephone interview will cover preliminary negotiations, but the contract will need to be discussed at the time of the appointment. There are a number of issues which should be resolved prior to establishing and signing the contract with each supplier.

The bride and groom, and, if appropriate, their families, should visit the site or place of business in person. They should meet with their phone contact and the particular person who will be assigned to their wedding.

During the interview, the supplier should be asked to provide a list of references. References are to be called by the bride and groom prior to issuing a deposit or signing a contract.

The unsigned contract is to have all of the services and costs listed, and the deposit amount and the cancellation policy need to be specified. The bride and groom take the contract home with them to read and discuss prior to placing a deposit. This allows time to review the contract terms. It also allows the couple to speak privately about the merits of the supplier.

Once references have been checked and the contract has been approved, the bride and groom return for their second appointment, with checkbook in hand. All questions should be answered by the business representative, and any unfinished business added to the contract. When the bride and groom are completely satisfied, the deposit check can be written, and the contract signed.

In addition to knowing where to go, it is also important to know how to go about dealing with the suppliers. For many couples, planning the wedding is the first opportunity they have had to negotiate with business representatives. The idea of expressing their own interests and concerns may not occur to the couples, but it is necessary for them to do so in order to achieve their desired end results. The vast majority of wedding suppliers are in business to serve the bridal couple and their families. They want to know how they can provide the services the couples are seeking. Additionally, the services can probably be tailored to the couples' needs if the supplier clearly understands what needs exist.

In those instances when it becomes clear that the only goal the supplier is determined to achieve is making a sale, it is time to find another supplier. This is also true when the bride or groom feels discomfort when speaking with the representative. Over the course of the wedding planning, there will probably be a number of times when the bride and groom must communicate with each of the suppliers. If there is discomfort during the beginning of the communication process, it is unlikely to expect that the situation will improve.

Sarah had reserved her reception hall and talked with the church secretary. She decided her next step would be to look at wedding gowns and check pricing.

Her first stop brought her extreme discomfort. Sarah wanted to look at and price the gowns, but the sales clerk convinced her to try some of the gowns on. Sarah asked the price, but the sales clerk avoided answering Sarah's questions.

Sarah had not previously encountered the sales techniques which induced her to sign a contract and write a one hundred dollar check for a deposit.

When Sarah arrived home, she was miserable. She had spent a thousand dollars more than she originally planned for the gown and the alterations required. She also disliked the sales clerk and didn't want to have to deal with her again in the future.

A friend encouraged Sarah to call the sales clerk immediately, before the shop had the opportunity to order the gown from their manufacturer. The friend reasoned that if Sarah was so uncomfortable at this early stage, dealing with the shop closer to the wedding would be even more stressful.

Both Sarah and her friend spoke with the shop in an attempt to void the contract and cancel the deposit. The sales clerk and the store manager were both hostile toward the young women. Sarah said she would not proceed further with the gown and never return to that particular salon. Sarah did, however, lose her one hundred dollar deposit.

Dot the i's and Cross the t's

A contract is a legal document, and agreeing to sign the document should not be taken lightly. If any portion of the contract is unclear or incomplete, it should not be signed until it meets with the satisfaction of the couple.

Both the supplier and the couple will want to have the wedding information and the services provided in writing. The supplier probably has a standard contract form to which she will add specific information. The couple and the sales representative will need to discuss the pertinent information and write all of it on the form prior to signing it.

Marie and Allen signed a contract with a major hotel chain for their reception. All of the facts were added to the standard form to the couple's satisfaction.

Several days later, Marie's maid-of-honor was scanning Marie's wedding file. She removed the hotel's contract from the folder and read it.

The maid-of-honor asked Marie if she had read the preprinted paragraph on "Acts of God". It protected the hotel from legal damages should the hotel be unable to host the wedding reception due to tornado, flood, fire, etc. However, the contract did not allow for refund of the couple's deposit. Although the intentions of the hotel were honorable, their contract had omitted a stipulation important to the couple.

Marie and Allen went back to the hotel and asked that a sentence be inserted and initialed by the hotel management providing for a refund of the couple's money should the hotel be unable to host their reception. The hotel complied.

It is necessary, for the well-being of both the supplier and the couple, that all the facts are recorded. Often the agreement to contract a specific supplier is made six months to a year or more before the event. It is impossible to rely on memory over that period of time. Additionally, should action result in a law suit, the written word takes precedence over the verbal word in court.

When To Rely on the Supplier

In some instances, a supplier must weigh his own need to express his creativity and produce a superior product against the needs expressed by the couple.

A photographer, for example, spends time photographing the couple, the bridal party, and the families. In order to achieve the desired results, the photographer will direct different activities and pose the subjects in different settings. These actions can distract the couple and lessen their enjoyment of their wedding.

When Kimberly was married, she had just returned from a two-year stay in Europe. Her wedding was an opportunity to be reunited with family and friends. Numerous conversations absorbed Kimberly's time, but she enjoyed the interaction with relatives and old friends.

Meanwhile, Kimberly's photographer was frustrated by his lack of access to the bride. He plotted ways to keep Kimberly from her guests. On two occasions, he took the bride and groom away from everyone to the country club's golf course for extended photo sessions. On another occasion he instructed his assistant to bring Kimberly from the dining area, through the kitchen, in order to avoid the guests. At other times the photographer was rude to guests, accosting them for conversing with the newlyweds.

Kimberly and Jim had not made a point of expressing their desires to their photographer. The bride and groom must communicate expectations to the photographer in advance. If it is more important for the couple to have the freedom to enjoy their wedding day than to have the photographs later, the photographer needs to know.

When aware of the couple's feelings and desires, the photographer may be able to offer other options to posed photographs. He may encourage the couple to have more candid photos in their album. The candid shots do not consume the amount of time as do posed photographs.

The photographer may also take advantage of unscheduled time, before the ceremony or during the reception for the majority of posed photographs.

Joan and Bill planned their wedding at a beautiful banquet facility in the country. The facility had originally been a private residence, but was converted to a banquet center as a memorial to the late owner. The building and grounds emanated character.

The couple planned to be married by a Justice of the Peace on Sunday morning. The schedule allowed for the key persons to spend Saturday night at a hotel near the facility.

During the interview with the photographer, it became apparent that early Sunday morning was an excellent time to take the posed shots of the couple, their attendants, and their parents. At that time, there would be less activity in the building and on the grounds. Additionally, the posed shots would be taken prior to the arrival of the guests.

Joan had no objection to spending time prior to the ceremony with Bill. In fact, the couple agreed that they would remain more calm if they were together and having the time occupied by the photo session.

When communicating their desires with the different suppliers, the couple should communicate the style, needs, and direction of each of the key wedding day suppliers. It is even more helpful if those suppliers who must interact communicate directly with one another.

The florist may need to speak with the baker if flowers are to be added to the cake. The florist may also need to communicate with the ceremony and reception facility caretakers in regards to the delivery requirements.

The banquet facility may need to be contacted by the baker regarding the delivery and setup of the cake and by the band regarding the outlets and setup.

The couple can ask that the photographer and videographer, once chosen, communicate with one another prior to the wedding. It is helpful if these two are aware of each other's style. While they need not work directly with one another, cooperation between the two is necessary.

Martha chose a young woman whose work she greatly admired to videotape her wedding, and a photographer from a highly regarded local studio.

The two artists met for the first time at the bride's home the morning of the wedding. The moment the two were in the same room, it was obvious their personalities clashed. While the young woman remained professional in her dealings with the photographer, he did not reciprocate.

At several important events, such as the interaction between the bride and her parents at their home, and during the cutting of the cake, the photographer deliberately positioned himself between the video camera and the bride.

The young woman made every attempt to alter this behavior, or at least to let it occur without notice. Martha, however, was aware of the photographer's behavior, and she allowed it to distract from her celebration. While she couldn't bring herself to say anything to the man she had hired, she did worry that he was ruining the videotape.

The more directly the lines of communication are established prior to the wedding, the more adequately they will work on the day of the celebration. A wedding brings so many personalities together, and emotions are so high, that good communication skills are essential.

A wedding supplier who is aware of the needs and desires of the client will be able to direct the situation in such a way that his goal of an excellent product in which he and his client can take pride is achieved.

Candi had clipped the gowns she liked from her bridal magazines prior to her appointment at the local bridal salon. All of the gowns had a similar cut, and all of the gowns looked great on the tall, willowy models in the magazine. Candi could be a very attractive bride, with the right gown, and yet the ones she had chosen were obviously not the right style for Candi.

Ms. Harper, of the bridal salon, was an experienced sales representative who had developed a good eye, as well as the tact required to communicate with the enthusiastic bride-to-be.

A couple of the gowns Candi had chosen were presented to her initially. As she stood before the mirror attired in one of the gowns, Ms. Harper carefully discussed how the lines of the gowns were affecting Candi's appearance. She gently mentioned how a different cut would be superior to the one Candi presently modeled.

With Ms. Harper's guidance, Candi was soon discussing the overall look she hoped to achieve and the amount of money she was able to spend.

Once the discussion was open, Ms. Harper was able to offer Candi a few choices which flattered her body type, gave her the appearance she was trying to achieve, and stayed within her budget.

At the conclusion of the appointment, Candi was thrilled with her choice, and Ms. Harper would be proud to have the bride tell her wedding guests that the gown was chosen at Ms. Harper's salon.

Use Your Creativity

There are times when even the best supplier is unable to help a couple fulfill their needs. At that point the couple must rely on their own creativity to achieve their desired result.

Maria found her ideal wedding gown. It was everything she had ever wanted, but the cost was four times more than she was prepared to spend. Additionally, she wanted a younger version of the gown produced for her six-year-old niece, Mia, who was to be in the bridal party.

Maria knew that neither she, nor her sister, Mia's mother, would be able to afford such gowns. The idea occurred to Maria that she would be able to find a pattern, or a designer, to create a gown very similar to the one she loved. With the liberty to choose a less expensive fabric, and by eliminating alteration costs and having the beadwork sewn into place by her sister, Maria would be able to have the two gowns for less than the cost of the one she had seen at the salon.

This alternative worked to Maria's satisfaction, because she was able to find competent, inexpensive sources for the work. As with all suppliers, references should be requested and checked. Thorough research will however usually produce the best quality for the price.

Another example of a creative option is choosing to wear a previously worn gown. This can be a gown purchased and worn by the bride's mother, future mother-in-law, special relative, or friend. Since most styles are compatible with today's look, this is a cost-saving opportunity.

Chris had always put her career first. She had worked hard to achieve her PhD degree and to establish her medical practice. She had little time for romance along the way. Then in her early forties, Chris met Ron. She was at a point in her life where she could ease up a little on her career. Chris found she was able to spend quality time with Ron and his two children.

After two years of dating, Chris and Ron announced their engagement. Of course Chris' family was excited and wanted an extravagant wedding. Ron was hesitant because he had already experienced a big wedding. He wanted something more private.

Chris did want a huge celebration, but was a little uncomfortable with the idea of being a bride because of her age and her community status. Her vision of a bride was of a twenty-year-old woman surrounded by satin and lace.

A compromise was found for the wedding. The couple and their families decided the wedding would be a private ceremony in the chapel of Chris' church. The celebration following would include numerous family members, friends, and business associates. It would be the extravaganza Chris' parents wanted.

Chris, however, was still uncomfortable playing the role of bride. She did look at gowns and suits at the local salon, but couldn't find a comfortable style.

It was Chris' mother who found the solution. She had been married in the forties, when Chris' father returned from war. Her wedding gown was simple, but elegant, and was made of pale blue satin.

Chris tried the gown and knew immediately that this was the solution to her problem. She felt sophisticated and mature, yet the gown allowed her the emotional attachment a younger bride might feel toward her parents.

Only minor alterations were needed, and a hat was designed to accessorize the gown. Chris was a beautiful bride.

Many couples are finding that by discussing their ideas with various suppliers, as well as family and friends, they are able to create a solution to their dilemma and set their wedding apart from the many others. Any part of the wedding can be personalized.

For example, Tiffany wanted to be surrounded with flowers at her garden wedding. She was married under an arch of flowers and had beautiful arrangements placed in various strategic places. She had a rose tagged with a beautiful card displaying the names of the bride and groom and their wedding date placed on the plate of each female guest.

As an added touch, Tiffany had the long stems of the toasting goblets decorated with miniature flowers and long ribbons in her wedding colors. The ribbons tied the bride and groom's goblets together to signify their union.

Variations on the traditional wedding music can creatively add a different ambience to the wedding ceremony.

During their ceremony, Susan and Don had traditional organ music played for all but one song. During the lighting of the unity candle, a harpist performed the special number.

Wendy and Kyle had a french horn accompany the organ rather than a vocalist.

Roberta asked her cousin to sing while accompanied by piano music for some of the numbers and taped music during others. Her processional and recessional were accompanied by taped music of her favorite songs.

Melissa had a song writer produce a song exclusively for her and Rob. The writer interviewed the couple about their special qualities and then wrote a song that was theirs alone. The song was performed at their ceremony.

Rhonda told her church that she was going to forego the traditional wedding program for the ceremony. She and Ted would have only the very basic ceremony, lasting twenty minutes at the most. Rhonda felt the ceremony did not warrant a program.

While discussing the matter with her bridal consultant, Rhonda realized there was information she wanted to distribute to her guests. Together, the consultant and Rhonda wrote a program for the reception.

The program had a border of roses to match the rose on the place card. It listed the names of the attendants and parents; the menu provided; the schedule of events, including the songs to be performed for the first and second dances; a thank you to their parents and a thank you to their guests; their new address; and a poem asking the guests to sing a love song rather than clink their glasses if they wanted the couple to kiss.

There are couples whose unusual circumstances require them to find creative ways to celebrate their marriages.

Rod and Ann decided to be married in the Bahamas to avoid pre-wedding stress. While they wanted their ceremony to be private, they did wish to have a party with their families and friends as guests.

They contacted a local hotel to arrange a tropical party to celebrate their marriage. The hotel placed umbrella tables around their pool. They served tropical drinks at pool side and served dinner under a tent just outdoors.

Guests were asked to come attired in swimwear. They enjoyed the steel drum band, the pool, and the patio at the wedding celebration.

Jan and Tim had been married twice previously and had been living together for over a year. The children of each were between the ages of ten and seventeen and all were impatient to have the couple married. Planning the wedding required some creative thinking.

The couple knew they didn't want a traditional wedding. They also knew the thought of planning such an event would become very complicated with the involvement of the children. Add to that the opinions of family and friends and Tim and Jan were distraught with the idea of a wedding.

The idea occurred to them that they could have a surprise wedding. Jan told family and friends that she was planning a surprise birthday party for Tim. She set the date and told everyone to dress elegantly for the occasion.

Meanwhile, Tim and Jan arranged for a Justice of the Peace to marry them during the party. While the guests thought Tim was to be surprised by his party, they were all instead surprised to be witnessing a wedding.

Molly and Pat planned to be married at her alma mater, Notre Dame. Molly was proud of her school and her heritage. She decided to have an Irish wedding.

Molly had shamrocks added to her gown and headpiece. All of the wedding stationery had either the sketch of the chapel where they would be wed, the school blue and gold, or shamrocks.

For the reception, Molly chose a pub where Irish cuisine would be served. The decorations were blue and gold with shamrocks added everywhere.

Bagpipes and later an Irish folk group provided the music.

The addition of a rainbow with the pot of gold at the end provided a special touch.

In each situation, the key element was for the bride and groom to first know what it was they wanted for their wedding, and then to work with others to achieve their desired result.

By communicating first with one another, then their families, and finally their various suppliers, the couples were able to achieve their very own dream of a perfect wedding.

6

Specific
Supplier
Solutions

Information must be gained, negotiations conducted, and requirements satisfied prior to engaging each particular wedding supplier. A contract is not to be finalized until the supplier has provided sufficient evidence that the services rendered will be to the specifications and satisfaction of the bride and groom.

It seems as if the search for suppliers never ends. Once one supplier is found and the contract negotiated, it's time to find another.

Ceremony and Reception

Most couples begin the supplier selection process by researching their ceremony and reception sites. Contracting for these two determines the date and locations of the wedding, establishing a framework to be filled in by other suppliers.

Often there is no question about the ceremony site. Because of the religious background of either the bride or groom, or one of their parents, the site of the ceremony is predetermined.

The secretary of the religious organization will provide information regarding availability of the facility,

88 Dream Weddings Do Come True

restrictions, regulations, and costs pertaining to its use and will schedule an appointment with the officiant for the couple to communicate specific details.

Many religious organizations require some form of premarriage counseling. The requirements for the counseling are set by the religious body or the officiant and vary in nature and length. There are organizations which conduct group engagement classes in the evenings or over a weekend. Other groups require that the couple meet with the officiant for a predetermined number of hours over a set period of time.

In addition to the requirements and restrictions of the religious organization, the couple will be given a schedule of fees for the use of the facility and its personnel, fixtures, and furnishings.

In most cases, there will be a predetermined honorarium for the officiant, the organist, and soloist. There will also be a fee for the use of the building and its maintenance after the wedding.

Many facilities include their wedding hostess as a requirement for weddings. The purpose of the hostess is to protect the facility from misuse and to serve the wedding parties' needs as they may arise. A fee will be imposed by the facility for the services of the hostess.

Kirk and Maureen were required to purchase the services of the wedding hostess assigned to Kirk's church. Maureen was pleased that she could rely on someone to direct the wedding party on the afternoon of her wedding, because she knew no one had been listening to instructions at the rehearsal.

On the day of the wedding, the wedding hostess gathered the bridesmaids in one room and the groomsmen in another. She alerted them to the proper times for their entrances, placed them in order for the receiving line, and helped gather them for photographs before leaving the church.

As the wedding party left the building, the hostess held the door for their exit. She closed the doors behind them and remained in place as the birdseed was tossed at the bride and groom.

Up to this point the hostess was able to accommodate the wedding party while protecting the church from misuse. She had warned the wedding attendants that once they left the building, they could not return, but Maureen's maid-of-honor had not listened. After standing amidst the flying birdseed, the maid-of-honor remembered that her purse was inside the church, and she tried to retrieve it.

The wedding hostess politely blocked the door. She explained that the church allowed guests to toss birdseed at the wedding couple only with the understanding that no one could re-enter the facility. The maid-of-honor waited outdoors, and the wedding hostess sent the janitor to fetch the purse.

There are religious facilities which allow the flexibility to choose one's own officiant and musicians. Most often the outside officiant will work with rather than replace the facility's leader.

Louise and Stephen were planning their mixed-faith wedding in Louise's Methodist church. While Stephen's family had no affiliation with a synagogue, they wanted a rabbi to officiate at their son's wedding.

Louise and her mother understood the desire of Stephen's mother to include their heritage and religion, but they were skeptical about their minister's acceptance of the idea.

Louise and her mother made an appointment with their minister to address the issue, but they truly thought they might have to disappoint Stephen's mother or move the wedding to another location. Neither outcome appealed to the two women.

At their appointment, they found that their minister was not only open to the idea, but very accommodating. He provided the name and phone number for a rabbi residing locally with whom he had worked previously.

If a facility allows the selection of an outside organist most likely the musician will have to be approved by the house organist. The house organist is usually paid for the time spent during the selection process.

Other musicians and the selection of music will also need to be approved by the officiant. Many religious organizations have set standards for the music to be played at weddings.

If the bride and groom, or their families, are not members of a church or synagogue, a ceremony site must be located and inspected, just as with the other wedding suppliers.

There are some religious facilities which open their doors to non-members. These couples must follow the same requirements as the members and sometimes pay a slightly higher fee.

Numerous non-religious wedding sites are also available. These facilities are operated like other wedding supply businesses, with specific fees and requirements. Historical sites, park district buildings or gazebos, private residences, banquet facilities, boats, hotels, or any number of locations can serve as delightful wedding settings.

The bride and groom must interview the caretaker of the facility and determine what services are provided, the length of time the facility is available, what fees must be paid, what services are offered, and the restrictions or regulations established by the facility.

Once the ceremony facility has been chosen and dates have been determined, the reception site may be secured.

The largest portion of wedding dollars will probably be spent for the reception. It is very important, therefore, that the couple secure quality service for their reception dollars.

There are two aspects to consider when selecting a reception facility. One is the actual physical facility and the other is the food and beverage to be served.

The physical building can be inspected for size, types of tables, dance floor dimensions, rest room accommodations, outlets for the D.J. or band, decor, and cleanliness. Additionally, the facility should be rated by its distance from the ceremony, parking space and availability of valet, and how it addresses special needs, such as handicapped, elderly, children.

It would be beneficial to know if there is a secure location for wedding gifts. The availability of a changing room for the bride should also be known.

Inquire as to other events booked at the facility on the same date. Ask where, within the facility, the events will occur and how they might distract from the reception.

The quality of the food can only be determined by tasting from the menu. Should the facility have a public restaurant, the management need not be aware that you are sampling their selections.

Some banquet facilities do offer a tasting, while others are reluctant due to the additional trouble and expense. Question the sales representative as to how the food can be sampled prior to placing a deposit with the company. Ask for references who can be contacted to discuss their satisfaction with the facility's food presentation.

Once the references have been checked, food has been sampled, and the facility has been inspected, request written confirmation of the agreement. The contract should list the following information:

Day, date, time of reception (arrival and departure)

Number of anticipated quests

Specific room assignment

Room setup (placement of head table, number of guest tables, size and shape of tables, dance floor location and size)

Room charge

Hors d'oeuvres

Menu (Have it written in the contract that you will be consulted should food substitutions be made.)

Food charges

Charge for children

Time of food service

Butlered service

Description of linens and tableware

Bar times

Beverages included and cost of those not included

Cake size and description, if included (dollar amount refunded if cake option is declined)

Service personnel included and costs if additional

How service personnel will be attired

Valet service and charge

Time at which deliveries may be made (cake, flowers, etc.)

Deposit requirement

Cancellation policy and refund

When final guest count is required

When final payment is required

Applicable taxes and gratuities

If a rental hall is the choice for the reception site, many of the same questions apply as with the banquet hall, but there are a few additional considerations.

The kitchen facilities may need to be inspected to discover if they are adequate. The caterer may have specific needs, or if the family is preparing and serving the food at the facility, there may be other requirements for the kitchen facility.

Determine if the setup and cleanup is included in the rental price, or if additional personnel must be hired. Also inquire if a security guard or building manager will be on duty during the reception.

The contract must include information regarding the availability of tables, chairs, and other equipment.

If a caterer is chosen, there will be a few different considerations than with the banquet hall. One of the major considerations is the equipment that the caterer provides in the cost of the service. The pricing should also indicate quantity of food, whether it is to be dropped off or served, and specific costs for personnel and overtime charges.

Melinda's wedding reception was spoiled by the discrepancy between the amount of food purchased and the amount of food served. She had purchased numerous hors d'oeuvres to be served during the cocktail hour. The guests agreed they were delicious, but in short supply. Several commented that it was a shame enough food had not been purchased by the bridal family.

Melinda's mother made several trips to the kitchen between conversations with guests. She kept requesting that more hors d'oeuvres be served, but each time only a few more trays would trickle out. As dinner was being served, Melinda's mother discovered a stockpile of appetizers horded by the caterer.

Photographer and Videographer

The photographer is one supplier with whom the majority of the wedding day hours will be spent. In fact, the bride may spend more time with the photographer on her wedding day than she does with the groom.

Because of the amount of time the photographer demands and the amount of direction the photographer gives to the wedding day, it is important to choose a person with whom the bride and groom are comfortable. If personalities clash prior to the wedding, there are sure to be extremely tense moments throughout the wedding day.

When contracting a photographer through a studio, ask to speak directly with the individual who will photograph the wedding. Interview that person and view his work. Unless this specific request is made, the studio may show the couple a compilation of photos from all their photographers and assign an individual who is unknown to the couple until their wedding day.

When viewing the photographer's work, notice the care used in posing the subjects. Note the arrangement of the veil, if the men's shirts are tucked in, where the subjects' hands are placed. Check the quality of the prints.

Allow the photographer to give his presentation. A couple can determine an artist's preferred style by looking at the types of photos highlighted in the presentation. This is also a good time to discuss special requests the couple may have and evaluate how the requests are handled by the photographer.

The photographer's main concern is the end result. There is only one opportunity to get all of the photographs of the wedding day, and yet the bride and groom will have numerous opportunities after the event to view the photographer's work.

The photographer must balance the need to consume some of the wedding time posing the bride and groom, attendants, and members of the families, with the desire of those persons to enjoy the wedding day.

Discuss the photographer's style, establish your priorities and objectives, and then negotiate the percentage of candid and posed shots.

Many wedding photographers are currently taking a photo-journalistic approach to wedding photography. Inquire if this style appeals to the photographer being interviewed. This style allows the wedding album to reflect the actual events of the day and may require fewer posed shots.

Ask the photographer if posed shots may be taken prior to the ceremony. Many photographers are suggesting this schedule because it utilizes dead time, the key persons are all gathered, everyone is more fresh, and there are no guests attempting to take photos at the same time.

Spending the pre-ceremony time involved in the activity of posing for photos is beneficial to the key persons. The only objection frequently raised is that the bride is seen by the groom prior to the ceremony. When this is an issue with the couple, the photographer must abide by the couple's desire and take the posed shots of the bride and groom separately. The balance of the poses must wait until after the ceremony.

Speak with the photographer regarding schedule. Inquire how much time will be needed at the bride's home and at the ceremony site prior to and after the wedding. This information will be valuable in determining the times of the wedding and reception.

It is difficult to compare the price of one photographer to the price of another, because most offer packages with various albums and proofs. The negatives are usually the property of the photographer, but proofs will be included in the package depending on the number of print orders received from guests.

The contract should clearly state exactly what the couple will receive for their dollars and when they will have their proofs and their finished product.

Video is an entirely different medium than photo, and the bride and groom will need to hire a separate professional to videotape their wedding.

Similar to the photographer, a person should be chosen whose work has been viewed by the bride and groom and whose personality is compatible with that of the couple. Unlike the photographer, the videographer will not have a considerable amount of interaction with the couple and the guests at the wedding.

The nature of the video requires that the videographer stand back and absorb the action rather than stage it. Although many professionals do interview the couple and the guests, the majority of the videographer's time is spent behind the scenes.

The videographer, like the photographer, usually offers a variety of packages. Question if the price is for a single or multi-camera service. Also know how many microphones are used and where they will be placed. Ask about the additional lighting at the reception and its placement.

Inquire regarding editing policy, childhood photo montage at the beginning and honeymoon photo montage at the end, titles, music, and additional copies. Some videographers will offer a short version for viewing by guests and a complete version for the couple to keep.

A form requesting pertinent information may be provided by either the photographer or videographer. If not, it is beneficial to prepare a list of the key persons involved in the wedding, such as the attendants, important family members, and special friends, for the photographer and videographer. Alert these professionals to those persons you definitely want captured on film.

In order that the photographer and videographer avoid causing emotional crises, sensitive situations must also be reported. Situations of divorce, family feuds, or hostility between guests should be mentioned prior to photographing or filming of the wedding.

A timetable of special events is useful. Mention, too, any unusual occurrences, such as no wedding cake, omission of the bouquet and garter toss, a unique custom, a birthday celebration and so on.

Restrictions or special features of the wedding or reception site needs to be reported. Most churches and synagogues restrict the movement of the artists and ban the use of additional lighting by the videographer.

The Wedding Gown

The aspect of wedding shopping which many brides find to be the most enjoyable is searching for and purchasing the wedding gown.

The most common means for acquiring a wedding gown is through a bridal salon. Most of these salons have a choice of bridal gowns, bridesmaids gowns, mother-of-the-bride and mother-of-the-groom gowns, veils and other headpieces, shoes, and other accessories. The bridal salon's seamstress will alter the gowns to fit.

Since gowns from these shops are custom ordered and altered, a certain amount of time is required. A comfortable time frame for the purchase of the bridal gown is no less than sixteen weeks prior to the wedding.

Because salon representatives choose the major lines they wish to feature, the styles and price range of gowns available vary slightly from salon to salon. When choosing a gown you also choose the salon. The major requirement a bride has of a salon is service, and therefore a gown needs to be purchased with the shop's service in mind.

Be aware of how the sales representative behaves toward the bride and her attendants. Before considering a gown from a particular salon, speak with the seamstress and view the fitting and alteration areas.

Talk with the sales representative about the bride's preference in style and cut, the formality of the wedding, and the dollar amount budgeted for the wedding gown.

Prior to trying on sample gowns, be sure to be attired in proper lingerie, panty-hose, and shoes with heels the same height as will be worn on the wedding day. It is also helpful to have hair and makeup style similar to the wedding day look.

When considering a gown, examine seams, zippers, and buttons for the care with which they were finished. When beads are glued, the cost of the gown should reflect the less expensive process.

Before ordering a gown, check with the sales representative about extra costs for items such as additional length and alterations. Also inquire about the cancellation policy of the salon. Have all the pertinent information in writing before offering a deposit to the representative.

If the bride is budget minded, salons often offer sample gowns and discontinued gowns for sale. Ask the salesperson about availability and the salon's policy regarding these styles. As with the custom ordered gown, ask about alterations costs before finalizing a purchase.

Rental gowns are also available in certain areas of the country. When pursuing this type of arrangement, inquire about the shops specific costs and policies. There are usually rental and cleaning fees involved, as well as alteration costs.

Manufacturers offer gowns specifically produced for the rental market to distributors, thereby making the rental outlets more readily available. The benefits of such an arrangement must be discussed with the representative at the rental salon and weighed against the privilege of having one's own gown. The bride can then determine what arrangement best suits her needs.

Florist

The selection of the florist and flowers may require more homework than some of the other suppliers. It is difficult for most people to know every variety of flower, foliage, and herb available as well as how long they will stay fresh looking. The bride and groom should search for a florist who can give them this type of information.

Begin by gathering floral ideas from bridal books, magazines, and catalogues. Also conduct phone interviews with florists asking about the varieties best suited to the season, climate, or environment.

After conducting the initial investigation, make an appointment with two or three of the florists who best represented themselves during the phone conversation.

Cathy found that she was required to pay a consultation fee to the florist for the time spent during the initial appointment. Prior to writing the $35.00 check, Cathy requested that she have uninterrupted time with the supplier, and she gained as much information as she needed to make her decision.

Ask the salesperson for actual photographs of arrangements the florist designed for weddings. Do not settle for sales bulletins. Inspect the photographs for the general appearance of the flowers, their freshness, the color schemes, and the attention to detail. Request references and check them.

Determine the salesperson's knowledge. If it appears the representative knows the craft, proceed with the discussion regarding the types of flowers and foliage and the colors to be used for the wedding.

It is helpful to have fabric swatches from the gowns. A creative florist may wish to blend numerous colors to complement and enhance the color scheme chosen for the attendants. Additionally, the bridal bouquet no longer needs to be white. The bride may carry a bouquet as colorful as her attendants'.

Also inquire about natural colors rather than dyes and color-fast ribbons. Marsha's gown was ruined when it rained on her outdoor wedding. The purple bled from her bouquet onto her gown.

As with other supplier contracts, make sure all the details are listed, as well as the deposit amount, the due date for final payment, and the cancellation policy.

The contract should list descriptively the types of flowers, the sizes and colors, the types of arrangements, a description of ribbons, vases, balloons, and so on. There should be a schedule of dates, times, and locations for delivery. List a contact person and phone number for each location. Do not issue a check until all details are satisfactory.

If flowers are to be arranged on the wedding cake, the baker and florist need to coordinate their activities in advance of the wedding date.

Be aware of the color of flowers used with the cake as well as the bouquets.

Kimberly's mother insisted that the florist forgot the flowers on the wedding cake. Photographs proved the mother wrong, but the white flowers blended so completely into the cake that they were not obvious.

Traditionally, bridal bouquets were carried for their magical powers. While this idea is long outdated, it may be fun to add flowers or herbs for their symbolism as well as beauty.

Remembrance is symbolized by rosemary and wisdom by sage. Honeysuckle indicates faithfulness. Innocence is displayed by white lilacs, modesty by violets, and fertility and happiness by orange blossoms.

It is customary to honor special guests with flowers. Also, the bride and groom often present each set of parents with a single rose during the wedding ceremony. Flowers can be added to the unity candle or carried during the presentation of gifts before Holy Communion.

The colors and fragrances of the flowers and foliage add to the ambiance of a wedding and can enhance the photographs and videotape for future enjoyment.

Music

The music creates the mood of the wedding day. People are affected by the sounds around them, and the wedding music can work to uplift or relax. It can create a soft romantic mood or it can get the party moving.

Organ music is the most popular sound at wedding ceremonies, although piano, guitar, brass, or string instruments may also be chosen. There are some facilities that have a sound system that allows taped music to be played, offering the bride and groom a wider range of sounds.

A vocalist adds sentiment to the music. While music is a moving addition to the ceremony, it is important to keep the music from drawing so much attention to itself that it distracts from the bridal couple. It is the bride and groom's moment, not the performers'.

Music is also a key ingredient to the overall atmosphere of the reception. The tempo and style will dictate the type of party which is being presented to the guests.

It is advisable to listen to various musicians prior to deciding on the ones to perform at the reception. Often it is possible to attend rehearsals, where the musicians will be happy to play some of your selections. Many musicians also invite potential clients to hear them play at someone else's wedding.

Be aware of the sound level and overall tone. Also note the tempo. Is it easy to dance to the music being played?

If it is a disc jockey being considered, will he tailor his performance to your individual style? Often a DJ can provide a performance ranging from outrageous to subdued, depending on your preference.

Most musicians will play special requests and direct the bouquet and garter toss. Make certain that this is the DJ's or band's policy.

First determine the banquet facilities policy, and then ask the musicians whether they will set up before the guests arrive or during dinner. Determine if they intend to eat and drink at the reception.

Make sure all the terms of your agreement are in writing. Include such information as:

Arrival time

Setup time

Number of band members

Instruments

Break policy

Attire

Band leader's name and notification should a change be made

Overtime policy

Cancellation policy

Policy for substituting musicians

As indicated earlier, DJs and bands often invite future clients to hear their performance at weddings. They should request permission of the bride and groom and tell the prospective clients to dress appropriately.

If this is an issue of concern, discuss the aversion to having strangers appear at your wedding and make note of your preference not to admit the performer's potential clients to your wedding in the contract.

Bridal Consultant

A bridal consultant is capable of assisting the couple and their families at any point during the planning stages, but the sooner a consultant is contracted, the sooner the benefits of her services can be appreciated.

A professional bridal consultant has a network of wedding suppliers with whom she works. They have been screened for quality and price. The consultant is able to ask the couple what it is they desire and the price they wish to spend. With sufficient information, she can direct the couple to or contract suppliers for the couple.

Choosing a bridal consultant requires some homework, but it is not a difficult task. One of the first requirements is that the couple are comfortable with the consultant, and the personalities blend well. There will be numerous occasions during the planning stages and on the wedding day itself that the three will interact.

References need to be checked, as well as qualifications and membership in a professional organization. A bridal consultant often must be able to think quickly and react appropriately. Experience is the best teacher in this respect.

Bridal consultants have various means of receiving compensation for their efforts. Many have a flat fee for each wedding. Others charge a percentage of the total cost, a fee per guest, or an hourly rate. There are still others who earn commissions from their suppliers and only charge for their time on the day of the wedding. The means of compensation should be clearly understood before a consultant's services are used.

Invitations

As the various suppliers are chosen, the wedding is being given direction. The overall tone and mood of the occasion is being set. The first indication the guests will have of the wedding's style is the invitation.

It is not necessary to purchase the invitations until approximately two to three months before the wedding. At that time the formality of the wedding will have been established.

When a formal wedding is being created, there is no room for deviation from the format of a standard formal invitation. The phrasing is established and the stationery color is either white, ivory, or cream. The size of the invitation can be 5 1/2" wide by 7 3/8" long or slightly smaller and folded once or 4 3/8" wide by 5 3/4" long and unfolded. The stationery is flat or may have a raised border. The print is raised. At one time, it was necessary that the invitation be engraved to produce the raised lettering. This process is still used for the formal invitation, but another process, thermography, also produces raised lettering and is acceptable. The thermographed invitation is less costly and more readily available.

Should a semi-formal or casual style be desired, there are almost as many choices today as there are brides. Also the wording of the invitation may be composed by the couple as an expression of their own sentiment. The invitation may be thermographed to produce raised lettering or printed so that the lettering is flat.

The stationer will have suggestions for wording the invitation, as well as the information on the reception card, R.S.V.P. card, and pew cards. It will be necessary to proofread all of the information to be printed and signed as to its accuracy.

Invitations are to be mailed approximately four to six weeks prior to the wedding. Eight weeks may be more appropriate during a busy holiday season. The envelopes are to be hand addressed in ink matching the printed ink.

Exclude the first names of the recipients on the inner envelope. Write the first names of children to be invited below the parent's names in order of age.

The invitation is placed in the inner envelope with the folded side down and the printed side or cover design facing you. The reception card, response card, pew card, and map, if necessary, are placed inside the fold.

Etiquette states that a response card is unnecessary because recipients will know that an invitation dictates a response. However, practicality tells the hosts that a stamped, self-addressed envelope and response card receives the most responses. A deadline date should be determined for the return of the response.

The response card will have an M followed by a blank space where the guest or guests are to provide their names. The names are to be written as they were on the inner envelope, such as Mr. and Mrs. Smith. There will also be a spot for the number of guests to be written. This number should be in agreement with the number of persons invited. When Mr. and Mrs. Smith are invited, the number of guests should not exceed two.

It is possible to have two lines printed on the response card as a clever reminder to guests that a no response is required if they will be absent.

Often there are persons who fail to return their response card before the deadline. These persons will need to be contacted by phone to determine their intentions.

Wedding Cake

The wedding cake serves three purposes at most weddings; dessert, decoration, and ritual. The bride and groom cut the cake and feed it to one another as the guests watch and the photographer and videographer record the event. Then it is served as a dessert or given to the guests to be enjoyed after they have departed. And finally, it is a decoration.

Because of the purposes it serves, the baker must produce a wedding cake with excellent taste as well as beauty and durability.

The cake is baked well in advance of the wedding. It will be decorated and transported to the reception where it will be highlighted as a decoration until after the dinner. The cake needs to remain moist and fresh until it is finally eaten. Additionally, the cake will need to support its own weight and possibly the weight of a cake decoration.

There are a number of sources for the cake. The reception facility often includes the cake in their banquet package. The caterer will also offer wedding cake as part of the wedding fare. There are bakers who specialize in wedding cakes, as well as the local bakery shop.

No matter which source is chosen, the cake should be sampled, actual wedding cake photographs examined, and references checked prior to making a decision.

Tuxedos

One of the last suppliers to be contracted is the men's formalwear. The father of the bride, groom, and male attendants usually rent their tuxedos.

The style of tuxedo chosen should take into account the style of the bridal gown, the formality of the wedding, the time of day, the season of the year, and the location of the wedding. If the accessories worn by the men are to complement the bridesmaids' gowns, fabric swatches should be taken to the men's shop.

It is useful to know if the shop carries their own stock of tuxedos, and if they have a tailor in their employ. If appropriate, determine how the shop handles unusual sizes.

Should some of the groomsmen reside a distance away, it will be necessary to secure their measurements for the tuxedo shop. It is best to send the groomsmen to a tailor in their town for measurements, rather than have them measure themselves. The tailor at the rental facility will direct the groom and bride regarding exact procedure for out-of-town attendants.

The contract should indicate cost of rental for the tuxedos and accessories. The pick-up and return dates need to be written, as well as the store's policy on damage to the clothing and their cancellation fee.

Transportation

Transportation for the bridal party can be secured as late as two weeks prior to the ceremony. While it is easily arranged, it is often overlooked.

Routing and scheduling needs to be determined for the attendants, the bride and her family, and the groom. The times which must be considered are routing to the ceremony, from the ceremony to the reception, and then the bride and groom to their hotel or the airport. Additionally, if the bridesmaids are driven to the ceremony and reception, the couple must be considerate of the bridesmaids' transportation back to their own vehicles after the reception.

The availability of vehicles ranges from the family car to a vintage vehicle, to a Rolls, to a horse & buggy, to a thirty-foot limousine.

It is necessary to confront a number of issues prior to reserving hired transportation. Consider the routing, the weather, the number of persons to be driven, and general comfort.

A horse and carriage may make a wonderful prop for the photographs, but is rarely a feasible form of transportation. A vintage convertible may also be lovely, but on a hot, windy day or in the rain, the bride may feel wilted before arriving at her reception.

When contracting transportation ask if the rental time begins when the party is picked up, or if the fee is portal to portal. The second pricing requires payment from the time the vehicle leaves the garage until it is returned.

The contract should indicate times and routing, how the driver will be attired, the insurance coverage carried by the company, the extras which are included, such as champagne, a bridal horn, and a white runner, and if the vehicle can be decorated by the attendants.

If transportation is not hired and private cars are used, routing must still be determined in advance. Each key member of the party needs to be assigned to a vehicle from each location to the next throughout the wedding day.

Each supplier has its own individual expertise, and the bride and groom must learn enough about each to make educated, intelligent decisions.

Research must be done, references checked, and all questions must be sufficiently answered by the wedding suppliers before the bride and groom can make their selections. Once each decision is made, all the information must be in writing before the couple place a deposit with the suppliers.

Through careful planning prior to the ceremony and reception, the couple, and their families and friends, can enjoy a pleasant and successful wedding day.

7
$\mathscr{P}$lanning
the
$\mathscr{C}$eremony

During the engagement period the couple will expend an enormous amount of energy in the planning of their event. Yet, a portion of the day, the wedding ceremony itself, is often omitted from the planning. In the rush to plan the perfect day, sometimes the reason for the celebration is overlooked by the bride and groom.

Religious Influence

If the couple is planning a religious ceremony, the order of events is often dictated by the faith or denomination of the couple. Each couple should have serious discussions between themselves and with their families as to the particular religion which will bear witness to and bless the marriage. In most cases, the religion in which one or the other, or both, of the couple's families worship will be the determining factor in selecting a church.

Although many of the components of the ceremony can be adapted to a couple's wishes, each faith has rules and regulations governing the wedding ceremony, and in many cases each officiant has rules with which the couple must comply.

There may be restrictions on days or periods of time when a marriage cannot be performed; requirements which must be met by the couple during the engagement period; certain rites, symbols, or ceremony to which the couple must adhere; restrictions on the music chosen for the ceremony; official documents which must be processed; and promises which must be stated for the future of the marriage and the subsequent children.

Elizabeth and Brad were trying to plan their wedding date according to the school calendar. Elizabeth wanted to take advantage of spring break. She reasoned that all of the wedding plans could be completed early, allowing the couple time to concentrate on their exams. They could then be married on the following Sunday. They would have two weeks after the wedding before returning to school.

Elizabeth's plan was fool proof until she talked with her rabbi. Elizabeth was informed that Passover was to occur during the time she had elected for her wedding. It would be necessary for Elizabeth to choose another date. Brad and Elizabeth altered their plans and chose summer vacation as the time for their wedding.

Rhonda and Cliff were to be married in the Roman Catholic church to which Cliff's family belonged. Cliff was not a devout Catholic, but his mother was very strong in her faith.

Rhonda had agreed to be married by the priest, although she knew she could never adopt the Roman Catholic tradition as her own. Rhonda did, however, love the beautiful facilities and thought they made a lovely setting for her wedding.

The couple were required to take pre-marriage classes and participate in a pre-matrimonial investigation conducted by the priest. During the investigation, the couple were asked individually if they would promise to raise their children in the Catholic faith. Rhonda was startled by the request for a promise regarding her children. During the pre-marriage classes, she and Cliff had discussed their views about raising children, but Rhonda had not anticipated the priest's request.

Rhonda responded truthfully that she did not foresee raising her children in the Roman Catholic tradition. Privately, Rhonda hoped that this would not prevent the wedding occurring at this facility. All the plans had been made around the ceremony at this church.

The priest restated the question for Rhonda. He asked if she would agree to raise her children as Christians. Rhonda was able to truthfully respond that she would baptize and raise her children as Christians.

In many cases, there is no consideration regarding a choice of location for the ceremony. The bride-to-be and her family automatically assume the wedding is to occur in their place of worship. This is often the least stressful option.

There are some religions which are more demanding of their followers. When a rite is to occur, the laws of the religion require that it be performed according to their rituals by their officiant. This often means within their facilities.

Locating a Facility

On the other hand, there are times when the couple are not affiliated with a church or synagogue and are required to locate the facility for their marriage. Or, they choose to conduct a search for a facility that complies with their desires for the wedding ceremony.

Laura's family had not joined a church when they relocated to the Midwest. Her fiancé's family never had strong religious ties. When it came time to plan Laura and Rob's wedding, they had difficulty finding an ideal location.

Laura definitely wanted a church. She also wanted a church where her pastor would be allowed to officiate. As Laura searched, she found that a number of churches only allow their pastors to perform the ceremony. A few would allow her minister to assist in the ceremony, but that was not satisfactory.

Just as Laura was beginning to consider an outdoor wedding or using a room at a banquet facility, she contacted a bridal consultant for assistance. Together they arranged a ceremony in the chapel of a historic village close to Rob's home.

The couple were able to use the organ in the building for the music Rob wanted, and Laura's pastor was able to officiate as she desired.

Just as Laura found it necessary to locate a facility for her wedding, Marsha, too, had to spend some time investigating the possibilities for her wedding.

Marsha's family had never been church members, although they did attend occasional worship services. When it came time to plan Marsha's wedding, she chose the local Presbyterian church for it's aesthetic value.

While talking with the church secretary, Marsha found that this church allowed only members to be married in their facilities. The beauty of the building brought the church more requests for weddings than they could handle. As a means to limit the number of weddings, they allowed only members to have a marriage ceremony within their facilities.

Marsha contacted a number of other churches and found each had their own requirements. Many of the facilities charged a greater price for non-members, while others, like the Presbyterian, allowed only members to use the building. Some churches allowed members to choose their date at any time throughout the year, while non-members had to wait until six months before their desired wedding date to register for their ceremony. Members were given first choice for the time of day as well.

After analyzing the different possibilities, Marsha enrolled in membership classes at the Presbyterian church and subsequently scheduled her wedding date.

Complying with Religious Rules

Various life situations will also alter the type of ceremony which is to be performed, as well as where it is to be performed. A second marriage is one of those life situations.

Divorce has become common in our country, and second marriages are inevitable. Each religion has its own way in dealing with divorce and a second marriage.

For the most part, the Protestant wedding service is the same for a second marriage as it is for a first.

The Jewish tradition requires that a person obtain a Get before a second marriage. The Get is the religious sanction of the divorce, without which remarriage cannot occur.

The Roman Catholic church does not allow divorce to occur among its members. As an alternative, annulment of the first marriage is becoming a common practice among Catholics who wish to separate and remarry. Depending on the situation and church membership of the couple, as well as the marital status of the Catholic church member, one of several situations may arise. Marriage may be forbidden by a priest, forcing the couple of a second marriage to be married by a Protestant minister or in a civil ceremony; the marriage may be performed by a priest at a side altar; or the ceremony may take place at the altar.

Donna and Bill now engaged, were both previously married in the Roman Catholic Church. Donna had sought an annulment immediately after her divorce from her first husband. Bill had not even considered an annulment until the time of his engagement to Donna.

As the couple began making plans for their marriage, Donna decided she wanted to be married in her church. However, the priest told her that in the eyes of the church, Bill was still married to his first wife. Donna was disappointed, but began making alternate plans.

Initially, Donna talked with the park district about renting the local gazebo for her ceremony. All she would need to do was hire a minister to perform the ceremony. While that plan was adequate, it was not what she desired.

In the meantime, Bill began working with his priest in an attempt to attain an annulment. Donna reported Bill's progress to her own priest and was informed she could be married in the church at a side altar.

With further consideration, Donna did not like the symbolism attached to being married in a lesser section of her church. She returned to the idea of being married outdoors.

Bill worked with his priest, who in turn worked with the priest at Donna's church. Through the efforts of all four persons, the annulment proceedings progressed to a point where Donna's priest was comfortable allowing Bill and Donna to be married in the sanctuary of the church.

Interfaith Marriage

Interfaith marriages at one time considered taboo, are occurring frequently today. There is, however, still the thought among family members that the person of another faith is different and a threat to the value system of the family. Some religious leaders see the person of another faith as an incursion upon established religious laws.

At one time it was impossible for a person to retain his own faith and marry someone outside that faith. As years went by, it became possible, but very difficult to have a religious wedding ceremony between persons of two faiths.

Today, it has become common for a priest or rabbi to be invited to officiate alongside a minister at a wedding in a Protestant church. The Roman Catholic Church allows mixed marriages to occur, but they do make the non-Catholic aware of the Catholic's obligation to the church in regards to attendance and rearing of children.

The Jewish faith takes different stands depending on whether the individual is a member of Orthodox, Conservative, or Reform sects. Orthodox and Conservative refuse to officiate at a mixed marriage. They view a mixed marriage as a threat to the future of Judaism. There are some Reform rabbis who do officiate at inter-faith ceremonies.

Marriage is forbidden between a Muslim woman and non-Muslim man; however, a Muslin man may marry a Jewish or Christian woman.

Mixed marriage is forbidden by Orthodox Christians' canon law, although the church does allow for abstention from canon law. As a result, it is possible for an Orthodox Christian to marry a non-Orthodox Christian. The ceremony must take place in the Orthodox Christian church.

When the bride and groom have determined who will officiate at their wedding, the officiant will provide an order of marriage. This order indicates the sequence of events and the content of each portion of the ceremony.

It is often possible, however, for the bride and groom to alter or enhance the order of marriage, by offering their selection of words, adding personal touches to the events, or changing the course of events. The amount of flexibility and freedom allowed is governed by the officiant.

Designing the Ceremony

Because there are so many decisions to be made and plans to be arranged, it is easy to leave the creation of the wedding service in the hands of another. However, the rewards of producing one's own wedding ceremony are so great, it is well worth the additional effort.

One benefit of creating one's own ceremony is a sense of pride in the end product. Through the ceremony, the couple can express their emotions for one another, their respect for matrimony, their feelings toward their families, and their regard for the guests they have invited to witness the event.

There is also the reward of having produced a unique experience through the effort of the bride and groom. Each will have had the opportunity to explore their beliefs and feelings, to express them to one another, and then to refine them and present them to their guests.

No matter who has written the marriage ceremony, there is a sequence of events which almost every ceremony follows. The ceremony begins with an opening; there is a message to or a recognition of the guests or witnesses; the words of commitment are stated; the rings are exchanged; a pronouncement of marriage is given; and the ceremony ends with a closing.

The Processional

The majority of wedding ceremonies open with a processional. This custom began at a time when women had few rights and were given to their husbands by their fathers. Historically, a father would bring his daughter to the waiting officiant and the bridegroom.

Some women are offended by the notion of being treated as "chattel" and do not want to be "given away" by their fathers. Others view the processional as a tradition which has lost its original function, but still adds pageantry to the event.

Gary and Barb were in their forties when they decided to marry. Both were being married for the first time and wanted a traditional wedding, but in their own fashion.

There were to be no traditional attendants at their wedding. Rather, they asked Barb's mother and Gary's father to be their witnesses.

When it came to the processional, Barb really thought it foolish to walk up the aisle of her church on her father's arm, but neither did she want to walk alone.

The couple designed their own beginning. They had the two witnesses walk into the front of the church with the minister. The couple entered from the rear of the church together.

It is becoming more common for the bride and groom to begin the ceremony arm in arm. Often the bride and groom will follow behind the groomsmen, who escort the bridesmaids up the aisle.

Another variation gaining popularity is to have the bride escorted by both of her parents, lending a suggestion of the equality of the parents through the processional.

Jill and Ted are planning to take the equality suggestion one step further. Ted will walk from the rear of the church to the front with his two parents just prior to the entrance of the bridesmaids. Jill will enter with her parents.

While the processional is the most common method of beginning the wedding ceremony, it is not the only choice. It is possible for the bride and groom to enter at the front of the facility after the guests have been seated or to be situated at the front as the guests arrive. In both instances, the ceremony itself will begin with the officiant's opening words.

There are religious denominations which conduct their wedding ceremonies during worship meetings. The bride and groom are seated at the front of the meeting. When it is time to exchange their words of commitment, the couple stand as a signal that their wedding has begun.

A Welcome Prayer

Once the ceremony has begun, the officiant usually welcomes the participants and guests. The Roman Catholic priest and Protestant minister greet the bride, groom, and witnesses. The Jewish ceremony proceeds with a welcoming prayer first for the bride and then for the groom. Other officiants may welcome or merely recognize the presence of the bride, groom, and witnesses.

There is also often a message given to the whole congregation regarding the importance or reverence of the state of matrimony. The message may be directed solely toward the couple. The message may be delivered in the form of a homily, sermon, or speech, and its length and depth are usually at the discretion of the officiant.

Choosing the Officiant

Many couples are married at the religious facility with which one of their families is affiliated. The officiant is usually determined by the facility hosting the ceremony. Most will, however, attempt to accommodate the personal desires of the couple. The person chosen to lead the ceremony may be a friend who has selected the vocation of minister, rabbi, priest, or judge. The person may be a religious leader who was an influence in the life of one or both of the couple. Some couples seek their officiant first and the facility second.

The couple may select an officiant in the same manner they select a wedding supplier. They make a list of possible candidates by asking friends of their experiences, noting the listing of persons in wedding directories who perform ceremonies, and checking directories of religious organizations. A phone interview with the officiant's secretary will determine who is available on the couple's wedding date, and who is open to witnessing the marriage of non-members of their organization. Once the list is narrowed, the possible officiants can be interviewed by the couple.

During the interview, ask prearranged questions about the officiant's opinions and beliefs regarding marriage. The officiant may also be asked how he or she expresses those thoughts during the ceremony.

Monica and Bill chose their officiant because of his experience with counseling married couples and his fluency when expressing his beliefs about marriage.

Monica had attended a wedding performed by Reverend James Michaels and was impressed by his words. As a result, she attended his worship services periodically.

When she became engaged, Monica had no doubt that she wanted Reverend Michaels to give the sermon at their marriage. She began regularly attending worship services at the Reverend's church and eventually joined his congregation.

Monica and Bill set the date to be married with Reverend Michaels. They also became involved in a cooperative planning of their marriage ceremony with the pastor.

Music, Readings, and Prayers

It is normal practice to include music, special readings, and personally selected prayers in the wedding ceremony, especially in the case of a religious service.

The bride and groom usually have the option of choosing their music and performers. Religious organizations often limit the selection of music to that which they deem appropriate. Restrictions may be placed on the style of music, the instruments, the vocalist, and/or the words of the song.

Donna and Paul had decided to have a guitarist and vocalist for the wedding. They chose works by two artists without complaint from their minister. When they suggested John Denver's "Annie's Song", they were denied permission. The minister would not approve the line, "let me lay down beside you".

Some popular choices for weddings are:

Traditional

Bridal Chorus from Lohengrin (Here Comes the Bride) by Wagner

Wedding March by Mendelssohn

Whither Thou Goest by Singer

Popular

Sunrise, Sunset (Fiddler on the Roof) by Harnick and Bock

Annie's Song by Denver

Follow Me by Denver

One Hand, One Heart (West Side Story) by Sondheim and Bernstein

Time in a Bottle by Croce

Day by Day by Berg

The Wind Beneath My Wings by Henley and Silbar

Because by Teschemacher and Hardelot

Through the Years by Dorff and Panzer

Could I Have This Dance by Holyfield and House

For All We Know by Griffin and Karlin

Speak Softly Love (Godfather) by Roto and Kusik

Classical

Wedding Anthem by Handel

Bridal March (The Birds of Aristophane) by Parry

Let Heaven and Earth Rejoice (Cantata 129) by Bach

St. Anthony's Chorale by Brahms

Ode to Joy by Beethoven

Jesu, Joy of Man's Desiring by Bach

The Wedding Cantata by Bach

Wedding Song by Schultz

Hymns

O Perfect Love by Gurney

May the Grace of Christ Our Saviour by Newton

O Lord May Church and Home Combine by Buck

The Lord's Prayer by Marlotte

Love Divine, All Loves Excelling by Wesley

Praise to the Lord, The Almighty by Neander

Ave Maria by Schubert

The readings and the persons who will present them may also be chosen by the couple with the officiant's permission. The readings may be quotations from religious works, or literary works taken from classical or folk selections.

Some possible selections are:

Old Testament

Genesis 1:26-27; (The creation of man)

Genesis 2:18-24; (The creation of woman)

Ruth 1:16-17; (...where you go I will go)

Psalms 100; (Make a joyful noise unto the Lord...)

Ecclesiastes 4: 9-12; (Two are better than one...)

Song of Solomon 2: 8-13; (The voice of my beloved!)

New Testament

Matthew 19: 4-6; (...and the two shall become one)

John 2: 1-11; (The marriage in Cana)

John 15 9-17; (...love one another.)

John 17 22-23; (...that they may become perfectly one,)

I Corinthians 13; (...but the greatest of these is love.)

Additional Readings

Kahlil Gibran, *The Prophet*

Elizabeth Barrett Browning, *Sonnet XLIII*; (How do I love thee)

e. e. cummings, (i carry your heart with me...)

Susan Polis Schultz, *Expressing Our Love*

Susan Polis Schultz, *I Promise You My Love*

Citadel Press, *All The Love Poems of Shakespeare*

Carl Sandburg, *Explanations of Love*; (There is a place where love begins)

John Ciardi, *I Marry You*

Eleanor C. Munro, *Wedding Readings*

Barbara Eklof, *With These Words I Thee Wed: Centuries of Writing and Rituals for Love and Marriage*

The prayers offered may be blessings or benedictions prepared by the religious leader. They may be written and recited by the couple as part of their own vision or blessing for their marriage.

Encouraging Participation

At many weddings, guests as witnesses of the marriage ceremony, merely observe the event. The bride and groom may wish to increase their guests' involvement in the wedding ceremony by encouraging their participation.

Encouragement can take the form of selecting hymns sung by the entire congregation, rather than performed by vocalists. Additionally, the readings or prayer may be presented as a responsive reading, where the leader and the guests read alternately.

In order to encourage their guests' participation in their ceremony, Don and Toni had the chairs placed in a semi-circle around the altar, leaving an aisle in the center. This was possible because only the immediate family members and their closest friends would witness their marriage.

The two had decided that their guests were an important part of the life they were about to begin and should be recognized as such.

The couple greeted and escorted each guest to a seat as he or she arrived. Once the guests had been seated, Don exited at the front and Toni at the rear of the church. Their ceremony began with a traditional processional.

The ceremony shifts from greeting and including the guests to the couple-centered exchange of vows. The solemnity alerts the guests to quietly witness the ritual.

Exchanging Vows

The bride and groom's exchange of vows expresses their commitment to one another. Vows are often written as a standard declaration for every couple entering the state of matrimony.

Each religious denomination will standardize the vows according to their perception of a person's role within marriage. A civil officiant will also provide their own short standard vows.

While many couples exchange the customary vows, there are others who write their own. By personalizing their vows, the bride and groom take the time to consider what they wish to promise. Frequent themes for vows include friendship, respect, honesty, fidelity, support, or growth.

It is helpful for the couple to plan with one another what it is they wish to receive from the other in marriage. This interchange stimulates discussions about what marriage means to each individual.

While repeating the same vows reflects an equality that some couples desire, doing so may not fit the bride and groom's individual philosophy. Each can say the words that most describes their own commitment.

These statements will have to be approved by the officiant prior to the ceremony, but they need not be shared between the couple. The vows can be kept as a surprise for the wedding day.

By writing and reciting one's own statements, the bride and groom will find that the recitation of vows will flow more smoothly on the day of the wedding. But no matter how well the vows are rehearsed, it is important to have them written on a small card where they can be read aloud should nervousness take over.

The Closing Elements

There is often a nuptial blessing, followed by a song. In many Christian ceremonies, Holy Communion occurs at this time of the blessing. In Roman Catholic Masses, the bride may choose to present a bouquet to the Virgin Mary.

There is a pronouncement of marriage and a final blessing. In the Jewish ceremony, there is the breaking of the glass.

Just as there needs to be an official beginning to the service, there must be an indication that the ceremony has ended. Often the officiant will ask the couple to face the audience and will introduce the new couple. The audience shows their approval with applause, and the recessional begins.

Traditionally, the bride and groom exit first, with the bride on the groom's arm. The best man offers his arm to the honor attendant and they follow the bride and groom. The remainder of the bridal party pair off and exit down the aisle.

Receiving the Guests

Often the bride and groom will have their receiving line following their ceremony. It is becoming more common, however to postpone receiving the guests until arrival at the reception.

The receiving line generally includes the bride and groom, their mothers, and the honor attendant. The mother of the bride is first to greet the guests, for she is the hostess. The groom's mother is next in line, followed by her son, the bride, and the honor attendant.

The other bridesmaids may be added to the line, following the honor attendant. The more persons in the line, the longer it takes the guests to be received.

The fathers are frequently included in the line, but it is not necessary to do so. When the father of the groom is from another city, he may wish to stand in the line in order to meet friends and relatives of the bride and groom who he may not otherwise know. If the fathers choose to be in the line, they are inserted at the side of their wife. Should one father be included, both are to be in the line. When the parents of the bride or groom are divorced, the mothers usually stand alone in the line.

Margie and Tod wanted to greet and thank their guests following their ceremony, but they did not want a traditional receiving line. They found the lines to be tedious when they had attended weddings of friends.

The couple chose a different method. They recessed the church and then re-entered through the side doors. Rather than have the ushers direct the guests from the pews, the bride and groom stood in the aisle and greeted guests one pew at a time. They began at the front with their parents and worked their way to the back of the church.

Wedding Program

When the bride and groom have taken the effort to plan their individualized ceremony, they may want to give their guests a remembrance of their efforts. A wedding program can be a useful guide to the ceremony, as well as a keepsake of the special event.

The program cover can be individualized by using a photograph of the bride and groom, ceremony site, rings, or unity candle. A watercolor of the bridal bouquet or a pen and ink sketch of the chapel can also be unique. The bride and groom may wish to have a special love poem or one of their songs on the front of the program.

The inside of the program can list the persons involved and the sequence of events. Additionally, the programs may be personalized by including poetry, readings, the wedding vows, a greeting to the guests, a thank-you to the parents, or an explanation of special rituals included in the wedding ceremony.

It would be unfortunate if the bride and groom poured so much of themselves into the ceremony and allowed the guests to be totally unaware of their efforts to individualize their ceremony. Having a wedding program can ensure that this won't happen.

The challenges of creating a personalized wedding ceremony are increased when the bride or groom's parents are divorced. There are both parents and stepparents to consider, not to mention the hostility that may exist between them.

Divorced Parents

When there is cooperation on the part of the parents, the ceremony can be organized smoothly. The mothers sit in the first pew with their present husbands and the fathers sit in the second pew with their present wives. The second wives are escorted into the ceremony site prior to the mothers. The mother of the groom enters just before the mother of the bride.

Toni and Rich were experiencing difficulty with Rich's mother. She was single, while Rich's father had remarried eleven years earlier. Suddenly his mother wanted to be perceived as a couple at Rich's wedding. She claimed that Rich's father should be at her side, because the two, together, were Rich's parents.

Rich's father, of course, had long been half of a completely different couple. He had no intention of abandoning his present wife for the duration of his son's wedding.

Toni and Rich had to plan carefully to avoid any situations which would necessitate Rich's mother having a partner. They had wanted the parents to light the individual altar candles, but found it necessary to ask only the mothers. The receiving line, of course, excluded the fathers. The photographer was made aware of the sensitive situation and was asked to avoid obvious references to the parents as couples.

Toni and Rich had to plan their wedding with care, but at least they were able to work around tricky situations. Many couples find so much hostility between their parents that it is almost impossible to proceed with their wedding plans.

The mother might expect the father to pay for the wedding, but not attend the special day. Other times, the mother may demand that a second wife stay away from the wedding events.

Parents need to be reminded that they are both important to the bride and groom, and the presence of both is desired. It is for that reason that the bride and groom extend their personal invitation to both parents. It may be the choice of one of the parents to decline the invitation, but that needs to be the parent's choice. When it is impossible to come to agreement, the parents may decide that one will attend the wedding ceremony and the other the reception.

Consider the Children

Children in the bridal party require special consideration as well. Their feelings and endurance levels are to be respected. If a child is terrified of walking down the aisle, or even a little shy, take the pressure off everyone. Let whatever happens be all right. Know that the main purpose has been served merely by including the child in the special day. It is always possible to have the photographs as a recollection, even if the child never makes it to the front of the aisle.

From considering the religious requirements, to the ceremony's recessional, there are numerous decisions to weigh before finalizing the ceremony plans. The time and energy you invest in choosing your ceremony events will become obvious to you and your witnesses on your wedding day. In the days and years which follow, you will be rewarded by the pleasant memories of your new beginning.

8
$\mathcal{P}$lanning
the
$\mathcal{R}$eception

The wedding reception, like the ceremony, has its own distinct character. The location, food and beverages, entertainment, and reception events need to be coordinated to achieve the desired ambiance. The couple may choose to make the reception formal, organize the reception around a theme, or continue the theme established at the ceremony.

What Kind

The number of guests and the formality of the reception need not be consistent with that of the ceremony. It is appropriate, however, to alert guests if a change of tempo is to occur. Separate invitations for the ceremony, dinner, and cocktails should be sent if the number of guests is to vary between those events. If a change in attire is to occur, the bride and groom can allow their guests time to return home. This information needs to be relayed in the invitation.

Maria and Rod desired a very small, intimate wedding ceremony. They asked their minister to perform the marriage ceremony in a small chapel located at their local forest preserve.

The chapel was chosen as a means of limiting the number of guests at the ceremony, as well as offering the intimate atmosphere Maria and Rod wished.

For their reception, however, Maria wanted to have a huge party. Rod, and all four parents, agreed that the reception was the time to celebrate with their friends, family, and co-workers. They chose a banquet hall to accommodate three hundred people and a dance band which would allow them to party all night.

Jill and Ted, like Maria and Rod, were also very private about their wedding ceremony. They wanted to exchange their vows in the presence of only a few people. But unlike Maria, Jill wanted to carry the same intimacy from her ceremony to her reception.

The couple planned a garden wedding and reception. They had a tent, elegantly dressed tables, a buffet banquet under a beautiful umbrella canopy, strolling minstrels, and an arch of flowers at the far end of the garden under which to be married.

The guests' invitations were appropriately written, according to the event they were to attend. A few arrived for the ceremony and the remainder for the reception.

The choices the bride and groom make during the planning stages set the tone for the reception. The site selected, the time of day, the food and beverages offered to the guests, the formality of the event, and the music presented create the ambiance. The list of guests invited to the event also affect the mood.

Most couples choose to subtly produce the mood. But there are some who establish an obvious theme to give a creative focus to menus, music, decor, and entertainment. Reception choices are made to comply with a geographic theme such as the tropics, a holiday such as Valentine's Day, or a sport, such as swimming.

Selecting Music

Music greatly affects the reception atmosphere. Soothing dinner music can be selected for the guests while they eat, while dance music can lead everyone into a joyous celebration.

If dancing is in order, the style of music needs to match the preferences of the guests. If there is a wide range of ages and styles of dance, be certain the band chosen can accommodate a variety of music types.

The musical preference of the bride and groom should not be imposed on the guests and expect that the guests will enjoy the reception as they should.

Ethnic dances and music may be appropriate, but will seldom accommodate everyone. Loud music with a heavy beat may be enjoyable to friends of the bride and groom, but may offend the guests of the parents.

Steve and Trina met at a jazz bar. They spent many of their dates at that same spot pursuing their mutual love of jazz. Of course, when it came time to plan their wedding reception they chose one of their favorite local jazz performers.

The couple's invitation list included some of their mutual friends, family members, business associates of their parents, and co-workers.

After dinner, it was Steve and Trina's expectation that their guests would dance and enjoy the music. Unfortunately, the only guests to appreciate the entertainment were a few of their mutual friends. Most of the guests visited among themselves, ignoring the performers altogether. Many, bored with the evening, left the reception shortly after dinner.

While Steve and Trina did dance and enjoy the band, they were disappointed that many of their guests were unwilling to share their enthusiasm. The couple regretted the fact that they had overlooked their guests' preferences in music. The oversight detracted from the celebration.

The bride and groom usually choose the song they wish played during the first dance. Often this is a song which has been special to them while they have dated. It may also be a song with lyrics expressing how they wish to live their marriage.

Mary and David wanted something special for the "first dance" at their wedding. They contracted a song-writer to compose their own song which gave expression to their personal sentiments regarding the day.

The songwriter asked the couple a number of questions, individually, and then together, in order to gain some knowledge about their relationship. She also asked for their favorite style of music. The couple chose light rock.

A song was composed specifically for the two of them. In addition to writing the song, the song-writer/entertainer recorded the number.

Cassettes were made of the performance and labeled with the couple's names and wedding date. A cassette recording was given to each guest as a memento of the celebration.

The couple danced the first dance to their own song.

The first dance is usually followed by a dance which includes the parents. There are several ways in which that is accomplished.

The bride may dance with her father. Perhaps they'll dance to "Daddy's Little Girl," by Bobby Burke and Horace Gerlach.

There are various opinions on how the dance schedule should be presented. Some say the bride should dance the second dance with her father-in-law, during which her father cuts in. Meanwhile the groom begins the second dance with his mother-in-law, and his father, having lost his partner, the bride, cuts in. The groom then dances with his mother.

The schedule can get very confusing. However the couple decide to spend the second dance, the bride does dance at some point with her father, and the parents all get involved before the dance is completed.

The third dance allows the attendants to participate. The bride dances with the best man, and the groom with the honor attendant. The bridesmaids and groomsmen pair off.

Finally, with the fourth dance, the bride and groom return to one another. The best man dances with the honor attendant. The bridesmaids and groomsmen remain together, and all the guests are invited to join in.

Menu Planning

Similarly, there are food and beverage choices to consider when planning the reception. Guests tend to base their level of enjoyment on how many of their personal preferences are met. When choosing the menu it is appropriate to accommodate the special dietary needs and desires of your guests.

Alcoholic beverages may be omitted because of religious beliefs. Similarly, the consumption of large quantities of alcohol could ruin the reception. If that possibility exists, the bride and groom may wish to limit the time alcohol is served.

Dietary restrictions for religious or health reasons also need to be considered. Buffet or family style meals offer the guests more control over their food consumption. A buffet usually includes several vegetable choices which should accommodate any food restrictions. The kitchen needs to be informed of the necessity to serve some plain vegetables. Butter, cream, or meat-based sauces should be presented as an option, as many guests may prefer to avoid them.

Brad and Rebecca had no special dietary requirements of their own, but were aware of several guests who did. Some of Rebecca's family did not eat pork, and Brad had a number of vegetarian friends from college. Rebecca's mother mentioned that several of the guests were watching their cholesterol levels.

To accommodate their guests, the couple decided to serve a family-style dinner. Rather than fried chicken, they requested baked chicken breasts. They eliminated the pasta from the menu, and substituted green beans almondine. Additionally, they asked that the guests be served a combination of broccoli and cauliflower.

To the couple's dismay, when dinner was served at their reception it still did not accommodate their guests. Bacon had been added to the green beans, and the broccoli and cauliflower floated in a heavy cheese sauce.

If guests are to be offered a plate dinner, it may be necessary to place special orders for a few guests.

There are times when even the most gracious guest is unable to eat around the offensive foods. For instance, a non-vegetarian may think he is accommodating a vegetarian with a plate of beef, vegetables, and potato. It would seem that the beef could be ignored and the vegetables consumed. However, the restaurant may serve the food floating in gravy, turning the vegetables into a meat stew.

Similarly, a person carefully monitoring their cholesterol, may not want the fat in the au jus on their plate.

It is difficult, if not impossible, to know each guests preference. All the bride and groom can do is make their best effort to accommodate their guests by discussing potential problem areas with the chef when choosing the menu.

How Formal?

Another factor affecting the mood of the wedding is the formality of the event. People tend to have different expectations and behave in a different fashion according to the formality of the wedding.

The setting chosen for the reception often defines the formality of the event. An outdoor reception, or a reception in a home or rental hall, may be designed to be very elegant, but the surroundings tend to be more casual. A formal or semi-formal reception most often occurs in a country club, hotel, or banquet hall.

The attire of the wedding party communicates the formality of the wedding. A formal bridal gown is floor length with a cathedral or chapel train. The veil is long, covering the train or going the full length of the train. Gloves are worn. The men wear a cutaway coat with striped trousers, gray waistcoat, white shirt and ascot for the traditional look. The contemporary formal look allows for more color to the attire. The bridesmaids and mothers also wear full length gowns, or the mothers may opt for three-quarter length. Gloves are worn. The difference between day formal and evening formal is only the time. Six o'clock marks the beginning of the evening formal wedding.

The semi-formal wedding allows the bride to wear a floor-length or ballerina dress with a shorter veil. The bridesmaids and the mothers wear the length identical to the bride's. The men wear a gray or black stroller for the traditional look, and again more colors for a contemporary look.

The informal wedding allows the bride a greater range of lengths; floor, ballerina, tea, or dress. A suit is also an option at an informal wedding. The bridesmaids wear the same length as the bride, and the mothers wear street length dresses or suits. The men may wear business suits rather than tuxedos.

The invitation is usually the guest's first clue as to how they are to dress and what they are to expect. A black tie wedding would warrant a proper formal invitation, and may occur at a cathedral in the late afternoon or early evening, followed by a reception at a hotel or country club.

Recipients of the formal invitation will be attired very differently than those who receive a casual invitation to an afternoon, backyard wedding. Similarly, their expectations for food and entertainment will also be different.

Kate was being married for the second time. The wedding would be Matt's first. Kate wanted to be married in a church for Matt, but she didn't want to plan a big wedding. The couple wanted to celebrate their special day with family and friends, but funds were limited.

The couple found, what was for them, the perfect solution. They had a church wedding. Kate wore a very simple wedding gown and had two bridesmaids who wore gowns from previous occasions. The men wore suits.

After the church wedding service, the bridal party changed their clothing. The bride donned white shorts and a white lace blouse. The groom changed into white slacks and a Hawaiian print shirt.

The reception was in the parking lot and the grounds behind a local bar owned by a friend of the couple. Drinks were served from the bar and food was prepared and provided by several relatives.

A rock band entertained, and people danced on the huge asphalt "dance floor".

The guests attended the church and party attired in shorts, jeans, sundresses, and casual slacks and shirts. Those in attendance, arrived at the wedding expecting a picnic-like atmosphere.

Seating Plans

The reception area largely determines the type of tables at which the guests will be seated, or if they will be seated at all, the placement of the bar and the band, as well as the location of the cake table and bridal table.

The bridal table functions as a home base for the couple and their attendants. It is a visible place where guests are assured of finding the couple. The bridal table should be set up even if the reception is an informal, stand-up affair.

The bride and groom are seated at the center of the table, with the bride at the groom's right. The best man is seated to the bride's right, while the honor attendant is on the groom's left. The remaining attendants are seated to either side of the four, alternating men and women.

The parents of the bride and the parents of the groom should be seated at tables which are visible to the guests. These tables are usually located a short distance from the bridal table. Each set of parents can choose the guests with whom they wish to be seated.

The parents best known to the officiant often request that the officiant and spouse be seated at their table. Grandparents may also be invited to sit at the parents' tables, or they may be given a place of honor at their own tables.

When parents are divorced, the divorced parents are given individual tables, to which they invite their own guests. Even when the divorced couple are amiable, they are not treated as if they are still married.

Introductions

Often the bridal party and the parents of the bride and groom are introduced by a Master of Ceremony. One common procedure is to have the bridal attendants walk as couples into the reception hall and to the bridal table as their names are announced to the guests.

The parents of the bride and groom are also announced as they make their way to their tables. They, too, enter as couples.

Finally the bride and groom are announced to their guests as they make their way to the center of the bridal table. Their table is frequently elevated, enabling guests to see them throughout dinner. The bride and groom enter the hall, weave through the tables of guests, and move to their spots of honor.

This event marks the beginning of the dinner hour. The introductions are frequently followed by a prayer, and then the toast offered by the best man. As an alternative to the introduction by the Master of Ceremony, the bride and groom may make the introductions during dessert.

The bride and groom can make their guests aware of the introductions, or have another person announce that the introductions are about to take place. The bride and groom stand behind each attendant. The one who has chosen the attendant gives their name, their relationship to the bride and/or groom, and what makes the relationship special or why they were included in the bridal party.

After the bride and groom have spoken about each individual attendant, they move to the parents' tables. There they introduce the parents one at a time, thank them, and give an anecdote about their own childhood or family.

When the bridal party and parents are introduced during desert, the prayer and toast mark the beginning of the dinner hour. The bridal party is seated, and the champagne is poured into the bride's glass, followed by the groom's. Then the honor attendant, best man and other attendants are served.

Toasting

After the guests' glasses have been filled, the best man stands and proposes a toast. Everyone is to stand at that point, except the bride and groom. The guests lift their glasses and drink to the bride and groom at the close of the toast.

Next, the groom stands, thanks the best man, and proposes his toast to the bride. At the completion of his toast, anyone may offer a toast, but it is usually only those persons at the bridal table who do so.

While the father-of-the-bride customarily offers his toast at the rehearsal dinner, Mr. Coldwell felt inclined to make another toast at the wedding.

Once the groom had offered his toast to the bride, Mr. Coldwell stood and requested a turn. He lifted his glass toward his wife and thanked her for bringing their daughter into the world, nurturing her into becoming a young woman, which ultimately brought them to their daughter's wedding day.

Special Moments

Weddings are made of special moments. The more those moments are planned ahead, the more fond memories the wedding day will produce.

Spontaneous moments to be treasured are also likely to emanate from vendors chosen to be of service to the bridal families. The photographer, the videographer, the restaurant manager, the bridal consultant, and the band leader or DJ can all contribute magical moments to remember. Their experience with weddings and the quality of their work also influence the wedding events.

Chris, the photographer chosen by the couple, recognized that the time had arrived when the couple were to cut their wedding cake. She ushered the couple from the riser on which they sat at their table to the cake table on the floor in front of them.

Often the cake table is placed in a corner and the bride and groom are photographed in front of the cake. At this particular facility, the cake table allowed access from either front or back.

Chris took a few of the traditional cake-cutting photos. Suddenly, she was inspired to take some additional shots. She called the parents of the bride and groom to stand behind the cake, while the couple cut the cake from the front.

Next, she had each parental couple cut a slice from the cake as the bride and groom had done before them. The overall effect was one of a new family being formed from two individual units. The photos and the warm feelings were greatly appreciated by all six persons.

Another special moment was created at Tom and Laura's wedding. The couple decided to cut the cake for the photographer and have the kitchen staff complete the slices. Rather than have the waitresses distribute cake, the bride and groom served their guests. This allowed the couple another opportunity to interact with and personally thank each guest.

Tom and Laura had a small number of guests which allowed them this opportunity. It would not be appropriate for a larger reception.

When the cake is served for dessert, the pictures must be taken quickly, as the cake is cut and served in a fast and efficient manner.

As the cake is consumed and the coffee poured, the band members prepare for their performance. Before beginning, the band leader will probably ask the couple for verification of the reception events and their times, and if there are any special announcements or song requests which were not previously provided.

The final ceremony, if it is included in the reception events, is the bouquet and garter toss. Some couples forego this event because they or their guests find it offensive.

Maryann and Roger chose to have the bouquet and garter toss at their reception, thinking the fun event would add to the festive mood.

When Maryann's pre-teen sister caught the bouquet, the family was pleased. Next Roger hurled the garter into the crowd where it landed in the hands of an intoxicated male co-worker.

The DJ had Maryann's sister sit on the knees of two of the groomsmen, while the co-worker placed the garter on her leg. He then encouraged and badgered the co-worker to slide the garter up the young girl's leg. He said the bride and groom's good fortune depended on his performance.

The situation became very awkward and embarrassing. Maryann's sister ran from the reception in tears, with Maryann trailing behind her. The bride's father also darted from the room, while the groom reprimanded the DJ and the co-worker.

Couple's Departure

In the past the bride and groom slipped away from the reception to dress in their going-away clothes and left before the reception ended. It was socially unacceptable for guests to leave the reception prior to the bride and groom.

Today's couples have put a lot of money and effort into their special occasion. Most wish to stay until the entertainers play the last song. As a result, guests tend to leave the reception as they are ready to go home.

Should the guest leave prior to the couple, it is appropriate for each to extend good wishes and a thank you to the bride and groom. It is encouraging for the couple to hear their guests recognition of the amount of careful planning the bride and groom invested in creating the wedding reception.

9
*T*ension
*A*reas

A wedding is an emotional time for the bride and groom and for the family and friends close to them. Participants may experience mixed feelings as a result of the wedding plans. Jealousy, anger, anxiety, and fear occur alongside the excitement, love, and joy created by the ensuing marriage.

Different value systems regarding finances, career, family roles, and expectations for the future become apparent during the planning stages. These differences may develop into areas of contention, giving rise to various emotions.

The wedding experience stimulates parents' memories of the bride's birth, the groom's first day at school, and their own wedding. Friends and relatives reflect on first loves, an engagement, future relationship, or any number of pleasant memories and hopeful thoughts.

Negative Emotions
Dormant negative feelings may surface or new feelings arise in those closest to the bride and groom, resulting in confrontations and conflicts.

The planning stage of the wedding can be a time when friendships are severed or family relationships become rocky. The bride and groom often find themselves in conflict due to the emotions being expressed by others.

If human beings were blessed with perfection, everyone would be emotionally secure, enjoy high levels of self-esteem and confidence, and love one another unconditionally.

Given we are human, we tend to experience inner turbulence, self doubts, and fear. We express those feelings to others in the forms of anger, jealously, hatred, dominance, and other negative ways.

Armed with the understanding of the need for compromise and diplomacy during the planning stages of the wedding, the bride and groom will be well equipped to deal with the stresses which will occur in their lives.

Mr. and Mrs. Williams had worked their whole lives to provide comfort for their children. Mr. Williams was employed as a butcher at a major grocery store chain, and Mrs. Williams worked as a bookkeeper at a local construction firm. They kept their expenses to a minimum in order to provide for their children. All three were given numerous opportunities to learn and develop throughout their childhood years, as well as tuition to attend the colleges they chose.

When Sarah, the Williams' eldest daughter had received her M.B.A., she secured an entry-level position in a computer consulting firm. Shortly after her employment, she began dating the senior vice-president of the organization.

Mrs. Williams remained cool toward Sarah's companion, Roger, during family celebrations, but she withheld open criticism of the man until Sarah and Roger announced their engagement.

Sarah attempted to plan her wedding with her mother's cooperation, but received nothing but opposition. Her mother objected to most of Sarah's decisions about the wedding and criticized Sarah's selection of Roger as a husband.

Sarah was hurt by her mother's bitterness. She realized her mother disapproved of Roger's divorce and the age difference between the couple, but Sarah was confident that she and Roger would have a successful marriage.

It was Sarah's aunt who made her aware of the possibility that her mother may have been jealous. Sarah enjoyed opportunities her mother never experienced, but until this time, all of those were given to her by her parents.

Now Sarah was making her own way. She was in charge of her life and was creating a very prosperous one. Mrs. Williams would never be able to give Sarah the kinds of things Sarah and Roger could buy. Mrs. Williams was interpreting Sarah's marriage as the end of her daughter's dependence on her for her needs.

Why Jealousy?

Jealousy generally arises from the fear of loss, including the loss of affection from an individual, the loss of control over a person, or the loss of access to another.

Parents may view their child's marriage as a separation, rather than a positive development in their relationship. A wedding is the time for a parent to step back from the role of teacher and provider, and to establish a new connection with their adult child. That new relationship may be uncertain and frightening for the parent.

Likewise, a future spouse can be jealous of the closeness which occurs between his fiancée and her parent. The fiancé could see his future in-laws as a threat to the marriage, because the parent and child have a history, a closeness, that excludes the fiancé.

This phenomenon is not limited to parents and children. Friends of the bride and groom sometimes display jealousy if they fear their friendship is in jeopardy. As the couple's relationship develops, the fiancé consumes great amounts of what used to be the friends' social time. Wedding plans consume the majority of the couple's attention, leaving the friends alone.

A fiancé may be uncomfortable with his partner's friendships. Friends have shared experiences, ideas, and dreams of which the fiancé has not been a part. Even while engaged and later married, the friendship may continue to include activities which exclude the other spouse. Jealousy can arise as a result of the apparent breaking of a bond of friendship.

Time becomes an issue when wedding plans place demands on the couples' schedules. It may become obvious to a woman that her fiancé is devoting more time than she would like to his career. She feels deprived of his attention or his assistance with wedding tasks. Eventually she becomes jealous of the time he spends at work.

He believes the extra hours devoted to his career are for his advancement and the financial security of his family. He would like her to support him in his career.

The reverse situation occurs when the woman is attempting to develop a career. Her fiancé becomes jealous of the time she devotes to business travel, preferring that she stay at home.

Jealousy can spring from a discrepancy in the amount of earning achieved by each person. This is especially true when the bride earns a higher salary than the groom. He could be jealous of her income or angry that he will not be the main wage-earner.

There is also the possibility of a parent or one set of parents being jealous of the other parents. There may be tension over the time the couple spend with one set of parents, the amount of money the others are contributing to the wedding or new household, the social connections the other parents enjoy, where the other parents reside, or any number of issues. These situations, too, can cause conflict for the bride and groom.

Divorced Parents

Situations of jealousy can lead to competition between divorced parents of the bride or the groom. One parent tries to purchase the child away from their ex-spouse. Or the parent may attempt to use affection or guilt to secure his or her control of the wedding plans.

Mrs. Rayfield was divorced eleven years prior to her daughter's wedding. Mr. Rayfield had been remarried for eight years and had two sons, Jason, five and Josh, three by the time his daughter was engaged. Jason was to be ring bearer, and Josh would also be a guest at the wedding.

Mrs. Rayfield established a series of events within the wedding to ensure her place of honor, over her ex-husband's, at the wedding.

Initially, she wanted Mr. Rayfield to pay for the wedding, but he and his family should be absent from the event. She said his present marriage was an embarrassment to her, and the guests would be confused by two Mrs. Rayfields.

When she lost the first round, Mrs. Rayfield didn't want her ex-husband to walk the bride down the aisle. When the bride insisted, Mrs. Rayfield said she would accompany them.

The husband's second wife usually occupies the second pew. Mrs. Rayfield argued that she should sit further back in the church with her three-year-old. The bride said her father would sit next to his wife in the second pew.

Mrs. Rayfield did not want her husband to have his own parents' table at the reception. She thought he should sit with some of his co-workers.

While the bride was able to override her mother on most of her demands, the constant competition made the bride's job more difficult and tense. The bride contended that many bridal couples have divorced parents. Precedents have been established for procedures, and wedding guests understand that one Mrs. Rayfield is the mother of the bride and the other is the father's present wife.

Spending money is another area of potential conflict. Each person comes to the relationship with a background of family financial habits from their own childhood experiences. Because the bride and groom have had different experiences, their expectations differ.

Budget

As the wedding plans progressed, Rhonda frequently found the services she wanted were more costly than her father had anticipated. Each time she approached him for more funds, he would grumble and turn over his credit card.

Rhonda and Kirk were also in the process of furnishing the apartment they would share after the wedding. Kirk had recently sublet his own small apartment and moved into the one they would share. He was uncomfortable about the cost of rent, but Rhonda wanted the new apartment so much he decided to grin and bear it. He thought they could probably be comfortable with their joint incomes.

Kirk had believed his bachelor furniture was good enough to start off their marriage. Rhonda had different ideas. As they shopped, Kirk would grumble, and Rhonda would sign installment agreements for costly furniture.

Kirk was displaying the caution with which his parents faced every major expenditure. Rhonda heard Kirk grumble, but proceeded with the credit purchases, thinking Kirk was like her father.

As Kirk became more nervous about their financial situation, he became more angry at Rhonda. He began challenging every expenditure she made. Rhonda began to feel like she was about to marry her warden.

The final straw came for this couple as they made plans for their honeymoon. Rhonda arrived at their planning meeting armed with brochures for cruises and exotic foreign honeymoon spots. Kirk believed they had no funds left for a honeymoon, but was willing to drive a few hundred miles and spend a short honeymoon at a nice hotel.

Rhonda was accustomed to her father giving her almost everything she wanted. She never considered what his debt might be like; she just figured he handled it.

Now Rhonda found herself in a position where she was unable to have it all, even while she was earning an income to help subsidize her spending.

Kirk saw himself sinking deeper into debt, a position he could not tolerate. What is more, he was incurring debt for items he did not want, nor did he believe they needed.

Eventually, the pain the couple was experiencing became too great for them to endure. They decided to cancel the wedding and recover what funds they could from the sales agreements and contracts.

Rhonda's father sent her on a cruise with one of her close friends, in order for her to recuperate from the ordeal. Finance is one area which needs to be discussed prior to the marriage or even the engagement. There are a number of styles, some totally incompatible, for earning, saving, and spending.

The first issue to address is the total income which will be earned. Will both the bride and groom be contributing financially to the marriage? If so, can provisions be made to live on one income should the situation change?

Will the couple establish a budget, allocating a certain amount of money to each area of expense and savings, or will the couple spend what they have when they have it?

What is the attitude regarding debt? There are some major items such as house and auto for which most people are willing to incur debt. What are the opinions of the bride and groom about credit for other items? There are some who believe they should do without an item if they cannot afford it, while others believe they should have the item immediately and pay for it when they have the money.

There are individuals who constantly think about their lack of money. No matter what figures are on their financial statement, they fear they do not have enough money. These people tend to horde money and spend little. They're always looking for that rainy day.

Others constantly think about and acquire items they want. They tend to buy without consideration of the consequences. They tend to be ostentatious about the items they have acquired, and rarely give thought to their level of income or debt.

Individuals exhibit both styles in reactions to changes in their moods. When the person is feeling abundant, for instance upon receiving a raise or an income tax refund, they will purchase appealing items for themselves and others. When they are feeling poor, such as when property taxes are due or repairs are needed for a major appliance, they horde their funds.

Some individuals have learned to live sensibly on the income they earn and adjust their expenditures accordingly as incomes fluctuate. They budget their funds and make regular deposits to their savings and retirement accounts.

Still others have developed a style where they spend little on themselves, but are very comfortable giving to charities, loaning money to friends, and purchasing items for relations who are in need.

The bride and groom need to determine how the other views their present financial situation and what provisions and adjustments will be made for the future.

Choice of Residence

Similarly, attitudes regarding housing need to be explored when the couple are contemplating marriage. If one partner has strong ties in a community and the other has a career which requires moving from one location to another on a regular basis, they will experience conflict.

The couple needs to explore each other's attitudes about the requirements for living quarters and the location. One may envision a ten-room house in the country, while the other assumes they will always rent an apartment, appreciating the low-maintenance requirements of such living.

Will the couple start with housing they have chosen together, or will one move in with the other? If one decides to move in with the partner, will they be the intruder?

Bill and Monica began dating two years after Bill was widowed. They both entered the relationship believing they would remain friends who just enjoyed each other's company.

Bill lived in a house he and his deceased wife had purchased fifteen years earlier. He had two children, a daughter, thirteen, and a son, ten.

As the years passed, Bill and Monica realized that they had become a couple and decided to marry. Monica was apprehensive about becoming the mother of a fifteen-year-old girl and her brother of twelve, but she loved Bill enough to take on the challenge.

Monica wanted to start fresh. She wanted to choose a house that held no memories and a community where Bill was not perceived as the widower.

Bill, on the other hand, saw no reason to relocate. He said the children were established in school and had their friends near by. His mortgage payments were low, and he was comfortable where he lived.

Monica's heart told her that she must start fresh, but her head agreed with Bill. Living in his house was the practical things to do.

After the wedding, Monica wished she had listened to her heart. She was haunted by the presence of Bill's first wife in every room of the house. Additionally, she had moved into "their" territory. The children never failed to point out Monica's mistakes when she did something different from their system.

Monica soon felt that she had lost her own identity and had assumed the role of the first wife and mother. While she had the duties and challenges of the first wife, she was not rewarded with the affection the children would give to their own mother.

Marriage takes on another aspect when children are involved. They instantly become part of the relationship, and often it is without the emotional investment the couple have made in one another.

How Children Fit In

Children also bring other family members into the relationship. If their parents' marriage has ended in divorce, they bring their interaction with their biological parents and grandparents to the new relationship. Often they carry the excess emotional baggage from one parent to the other, leaving it just inside the door of the new family.

When both the bride and groom have children from previous marriages, they must cope with the interaction between those children as well. Questions of discipline, family organization, and support of the children must enter into the planning of the marriage.

Children often wonder where they fit in a new relationship established by a parent. It is helpful to discuss their individual roles within the marriage and family structure as the wedding plans progress.

Insecurity

Another problem which may arise is a sense of insecurity on a part of the bride or groom.

Dave had been married for only three months when his wife walked out on him. He was haunted by her departure for three years before he met Lynn. While Dave originally believed he would never love again, Lynn won his heart.

During the initial stages of their eighteen month engagement, Dave was loving and cooperative, but as the wedding date came nearer, he was possessive and moody. Lynn was troubled by his constant depression and was annoyed by the lack of freedom he allowed her. Whenever Lynn wanted to go out alone, Dave argued with her. If she did meet her friends or run errands without Dave, he made frequent calls to her home until she returned.

Lynn was ready to break the engagement when her minister offered to talk with Dave. It was discovered that Dave was reliving his wife's departure and placing Lynn in the role of his first wife.

Dave was becoming insecure about the success of his second marriage as the wedding date drew near. Armed with this knowledge, Dave and Lynn were able to discuss his insecurity when it arose and make their relationship harmonious.

Insecurity may arise as the couple think about the financial obligation they have for their own support. The bride or groom may feel insecure about the role of wife or husband or may be apprehensive about raising children.

If each partner is aware of potential insecurities as they prepare for their wedding, they can better communicate their needs and work toward solutions.

Handling Frustration

When desire and reality conflict in the planning stages of a wedding, frustration may occur. Efforts need to be made to achieve the wedding the bride and groom want, but often compromises must be made in order to make the wedding a success.

Trina was determined to have a wedding different from the several she attended recently. She had talked with her fiancé, Ron, and he had agreed to follow her plan.

Sunday afternoon was chosen for the ceremony and reception. Trina planned to have finger foods and punch in a banquet hall. For entertainment, she desired classical music and waltzes.

The initial interview with the banquet manager provided Trina's first surprise. She discovered that the cost for her desired foods was very similar to providing the guests with a complete meal. Trina chose a chicken dinner.

While seeking entertainment, Trina was made aware that her guests would probably not waltz, and she opted for band music of the forties.

Trina was terribly frustrated that her wedding was turning into a clone of the many others she attended. It had not occurred to her that one of the reasons weddings seemed similar was that wedding suppliers had a tried and true method for accommodating clients. Over the years, each business had learned the most effective and acceptable means of feeding and entertaining wedding guests.

To discover that your vision of the perfect wedding has some impracticable components is frustrating. Many expectations are developed while planning a wedding, and it is only natural that a few desires will go unsatisfied. You need to be philosophical about the disappointments and revel in the successes.

The planning stages of a wedding are tension-filled times when there are more possibilities for disagreements than when the couple dated. It is beneficial to note the situations which cause the most tension. These may well be the same situations which will cause conflict during the marriage.

10

Dealing With Stress

The engagement period can be one of the most affirming times in a couple's life. Excitement, romance, and love are all around them. With so much joy, why are there tears, arguments, and depression as well?

The Causes of Stress

Stress is an inner reaction to the changes and demands occurring in our lives. Stress often obscures joy. Some causes of stress in the process of planning a wedding are:

Time pressures: too much work to accomplish in too little time.

Financial concerns: fear that there are too many expenses to be covered by available monetary funds. Also incurring large debt, like mortgage or car loan.

Fatigue: not planning free time for fun, or not being able to take a desired vacation.

Relocation: experiencing a change in residence.

Exhaustion: poor sleep patterns or poor nutrition.

Anxiety: change in lifestyle caused by loss of independence or addition to a family.

Fear of the unknown: career changes due to relocation or graduation.

Relationship tensions: assuming the financial or emotional burdens of another.

The Nature of Stress

While stress can harm us if allowed to, it is important to be aware that stress can also be good for us. Stress can be the excitement felt at the time of engagement, at the wedding, or moving into a new home. It is the gearing up for the challenges which come with any change. It is not the existence of stress which needs to be avoided, it is the failure to react to stress in an appropriate manner, using its existence as a catalyst to new growth and strength. Failure to deal with stress in a person's life is a major cause of depression.

The existence of stress or excitement makes us vibrant individuals, capable of joyful laughing, reaching, and striving. Some stress needs to be nourished and enjoyed.

Often the positive kind of stress comes with change and the challenges change brings. Preparing for a new life causes stress. The way the person reacts to and thinks about that change dictates whether the stress will produce appropriate or harmful results.

Eileen has always seen the cup as half empty, while Chris has seen it half full. Chris never allowed Eileen's negativity to bother him until they began planning their wedding. As they made plans, he noticed that she rarely faced a new situation or made a decision without complaining extensively.

Eileen saw suppliers as pushy and rude, while Chris noticed that they were efficiently helping the couple make definite plans for their quickly approaching wedding date. While Eileen was immobilized by fears, Chris and the suppliers were able to make progress.

Chris said the band had a unique sound, Eileen said they didn't need to learn their craft at her wedding. Eileen said the florist was foolish. Chris said he was creative.

Even though the engagement had limited their private time, Chris told Eileen he enjoyed their time together. Eileen said she was burnt out over all the family invitations they had to accept.

Eileen became more nervous and irritable as the wedding day neared. She focused on all that needed to be accomplished, all that could go wrong, and all that she personally lacked to get the job done.

Chris, on the other hand, remained calm. He was positive that he and Eileen had made the right decisions and would have the wedding they wanted. He also was confident that he could handle any last minute crisis that may arise.

Persons who analyze every new encounter as a threat and worry that the worst will happen experience harmful stress. It is their interpretation of the situation itself, rather than the situation itself which causes them harm.

Physical Reasons for Stress

Planning a wedding results in physical as well as emotional stress. The bride and groom are caught up in a hectic pace, trying to accomplish numerous tasks in a set amount of time. Social demands are placed on their time for pre-wedding celebrations. They are expected to appear at family gatherings so everyone can meet them, and, to complicate things more, there are two families.

There may be personal belongings to sort and relocate to a new residence. In addition purchases must be made for for their home.

Suppliers must be interviewed and locations inspected. This may involve the tedious driving, parking, walking, and driving again cycle which is often a part of wedding planning and shopping.

Poor nutrition may also be a factor in physical stress. Party food and irregular eating schedules cause the couple to overlook a balanced diet. One or both of the individuals may be attempting to lose weight in a short amount of time, which could mean when they are not partying, they're starving.

Sleep patterns are usually affected by the increased demands of wedding planning and social and family gatherings. A person who is run down due to lack of rest and good nutrition accomplishes less than a healthy person in any given amount of time. This causes additional stress, which in turn, causes lack of sleep. The inevitable, vicious circle!

Demands

Physical and emotional stresses are further compounded by relationship stresses which surface during the engagement period. Friends and relatives with emotional stakes in the outcome of the wedding often feel free to express their concerns and anxieties to the bride and groom.

The couple may hear some of their family member's concerns as demands when they are merely intended as comments. A mother may mention that she wonders if there will be enough variety in the reception menu. The bride may hear her mother demanding control of the menu planning.

The concerns of friends may also be heard differently than they were intended. The best man may say that he wonders if one of the groomsmen will overdo the alcohol at the rehearsal dinner and reception, as he's been known to do in the past. The groom may hear a subtle suggestion for chauffeured transportation or the removal of that particular groomsman from the bridal party.

It may be helpful for the couple to withhold their judgment of such comments, and to ask the other individual to elaborate. The bride or groom may find they are receiving helpful information and suggestions rather than demands.

Demands issued by family, friends, each other, and upon oneself should be examined. The bride and groom can analyze the demands and ask if they are within reach of being met, and if they are demands worthy of being achieved.

The couple may decide they are expending too much energy and accomplishing too little due to unreasonable demands. The demands may be causing the couple to spend non-productive time at non-essential social gatherings or overly abundant family activities.

The stress of excessive demands can be reduced by limiting activities. Some of the wedding planning can be done on the phone; some of the invitations can be declined; and some of the extras may be omitted. The couple may decide to take an attractive invitation rather than running from shop to shop trying to find an exact copy of the one in the bride or groom's mind. They may decide to pay the additional amount for the florist they like, rather than shopping continuously for the same quality at a slightly lesser price.

Some responsibilities can be delegated. The bride and groom need not assume full responsibility for every task. There are bridal consultants, honor attendants, best men, parents, and friends and relatives who would appreciate the opportunity to be of service to the couple.

Plans for the wedding can be simplified. It is possible to create the desired wedding without turning it into a major production. The bride and groom may be planning their one wedding, but the suppliers they have chosen have planned innumerable similar affairs. They know the shortcuts and are happy to share their expertise.

Self-imposed demands can be reduced as well. The bride can accept that she is not going to lose sufficient weight in a few short months to fit into a bridal gown two sizes smaller than she has ever worn before.

It is unlikely that the groom is going to invite three hundred guests and make each and every one of them one hundred percent happy.

The couple must assume control, knowing it is their wedding and they have a right to its design. So many people have opinions as to how the wedding plans should proceed, but it is the couple who are being wed.

The bride and groom can eliminate many of the "shoulds" and "have tos" from their minds. A parent may say they have to invite his boss's third cousin. A friend may say you should have a throw-away bouquet.

Accept these comments as advice and act appropriately for your desired wedding.

Sue and Paul had decided to invite only adults to their wedding. They were paying a substantial amount of money per plate for the dinner, and they could not afford to invite all of the children in the family. They also had decided that the evening wedding and late reception would produce tired, cranky children.

Sue's out-of-town cousin had accepted the invitation, but requested permission to bring her three children to the reception because she had no one to care for them.

Joanne, a co-worker of Sue's also requested permission to bring her infant because she was nursing him.

When Emily, Sue's sister, discovered there were other parents asking to bring their children, she demanded the opportunity to bring her two toddlers, arguing that they were immediate family.

Sue began to feel the stress of being out of control of her own guest list, knowing that each additional name added more expense and confusion. She needed to take control and offer conditions to the guests. Her options were to hold firm and politely explain that children would not be present; hire someone to care for the children at a conveniently located facility; allow the children to attend the wedding day up until dinner; or change the guest list to include some children.

Some demands are more subtle than others, as in Marsha's case. Marsha and Jim planned an afternoon wedding in order to save expenses, and because the celebration was of no major importance to them.

Marsha had decided to purchase a street length white dress at a local department store. She reasoned that she would save money, and her bridesmaids would do the same.

Neither Marsha's mother nor her future mother-in-law were pleased with the idea. Jim's mother kept trying to find a gown for Marsha to borrow. Marsha's mother perused her bridal magazines and marked the pages where flattering gowns appeared.

Marsha recognized the subtle demands, but was able to hold firm to her desire, until her mother took her shopping. Marsha had intended to look at attractive department store dresses. Her mother took her to a bridal salon.

As if the scene had been rehearsed by Marsha's mother and the sales clerk, three street length gowns were placed before Marsha. Her mother encouraged her to try them on. They all looked bad.

Her mother and sales clerk suggested that as long as she was in the salon, she might as well try a full-length gown or two. As the session unfolded, Marsha was caught up in the beauty of the gowns and purchased one that her mother liked.

Marsha gave in to her mother's ploy and then suffered stress, due to relinquishing her initial desire. She spent more money than she originally intended on her gown. Because it was Marsha's desire that she and the bridesmaids have the same length gowns, her attendants would also spend more money on the purchase of their attire.

The plans Marsha had made were altered by others. Marsha did not keep to her original idea and allow time to locate her ideal gown. To lessen the stress Marsha was feeling, she could enjoy the idea of wearing the beautiful gown at her wedding and learn from the lesson. Before agreeing to future purchases, Marsha needed to be certain that she was attaining her desire and receiving the best value for her dollar.

The demands placed on the bride and groom by the parents may become more pronounced when the wedding is being financed by the the hands of the parents, and therefore the decisions may also rest with them.

It may be necessary for the bride and groom to negotiate how purchasing decisions are to be made with the person responsible for paying the bills. Less stress will be incurred if there is a clear understanding how the wedding is to be designed from the start. Each couple needs to ask the question: Will the wedding be completely to their specifications, or is there room for compromise?

Conquering Fear

Fear is another cause of mental stress. When a person worries about an outcome, they imagine undesired results. The expectation of negative events leads to fear. Fear, allowed to flourish, causes harmful stress to build.

To fear an occurrence is not necessarily bad. Fear is an emotion which allows us to overcome dangers. Fear properly dealt with says take a look, analyze, and then make whatever corrections are necessary.

Marsha feared she and Jim could not afford an elaborate wedding, and the couple made the adjustment to a small afternoon event. She heard the message of her fear, took appropriate action, and moved forward in her plans.

Analysing the aspects of the wedding causing the most stress will produce a solution. Is the receiving line a problem area, or does the long aisle cause anxiety? The situation can be altered, and the anxiety relieved.

Emily was in terror thinking about walking down the aisle with each and every guest's eyes glued to her. She was sure she would stumble or trip her father, or her knees would fold and she would be immobile. Several times, she told her fiancé she didn't want to get married, just because the aisle was causing her to panic.

Emily's minister helped her to analyze the situation. He talked with her about all the different situations occurring during the ceremony. She didn't seem frightened to stand at the altar with the groom. Exchanging vows didn't scare her. Exiting the church with the groom seemed all right. It was just the initial walk down the aisle that had Emily in a panic.

Emily knew there would be a hush over the crowd. She had seen the guests stand and turn to watch the bride's every move. She even knew the guests pivoted as the bride passed them by. Their eyes held firm to the bride until she reached the front of the church.

Emily's minister offered a solution. He asked Emily if she would like to enter the front of the church from the choir room. The ceremony would begin with the groomsmen entering from one side of the altar and the bridesmaids from the opposite side. Emily was relieved and happy to accept the minister's recommendation.

Dwelling on negative consequences is nonproductive and stressful. Should the situation be within the bride or grooms control, fear can alert them to an unwanted or unpleasant situation, and they can make the necessary correction. Unfortunately, there are persons who worry or fear because they dwell on the unwanted results rather than focusing on a positive outcome.

Maureen's mother was a born worrier. It seemed that worry had become so much a part of Mrs. Flynn's life that she was worried when she had nothing to worry about.

Maureen was very organized. She and her fiancé, Dennis, decided on their budget, made their guest list, and contacted the necessary suppliers. They had a clear vision of the wedding they wanted and acted on that design.

Mrs. Flynn, however, had a need to find a flaw in each plan. She worried that Maureen had chosen such a different color for the bridesmaids that the florist would never be able to match the hue. She worried that the vocalist was not practicing with the organist. She worried that Maureen's father was not negotiating correctly with the supplier of the tuxedos. She worried that the wedding immediately following Maureen and Dennis' was scheduled too tightly, and that the wedding party would disrupt her daughter's wedding.

Mrs. Flynn was filling her mind, and that of the bride and groom, with visions of disaster. She was inadvertently producing unnecessary fear in the couple and causing harmful stress. Had Mrs. Flynn focused on the desired outcome, everyone would have benefited from the calm.

Learning to focus on the desired outcomes, rather than those which are not wanted, has a number of benefits. When the bride and groom are aware of the results they are seeking, they can better communicate those desires to one another, their parents, their officiant, the suppliers, and their guests.

Knowing what is desired and how to attain it helps to become more assertive about having their needs filled. With this assertiveness comes confidence, and with confidence comes less worry.

Decreasing Stress

Harmful stress incurred during wedding planning is decreased by clearly envisioning the desired wedding and marriage, and by making that vision apparent to other participants.

Barb and Dave spent their time together discussing how they wanted the ceremony to unfold, what they wanted to occur at their reception, what their expectations were for their honeymoon, their first residence, and their eventual family.

Barb found that when she was away from Dave she pictured them together during the different events the two had discussed. When she was driving to an appointment with a supplier, she would see herself walking down the aisle on her father's arm. Dave would calmly wait at the altar.

Barb daydreamed about the condo they hoped to buy while she was stuck in traffic on her commute to work. Every opportunity Barb found, she was envisioning different aspects of her future. She saw herself as a radiant, composed bride. Dave was confident and handsome. The ceremony combined their sentiments with the tradition of their religion. There was an aura of romance, love and joy. The reception was the best party she had ever attended. Barb's mind kept creating pictures of the results she wanted.

Friends of the couple could not believe how calm Barb remained during the wedding planning. Even when the couple hit a snag in their plans, Barb was able to approach the situation with calm assurance.

Barb did not realize that her daydreams were fostering confidence and relieving stress. She had accidentally found a method of relaxation and was using it to her benefit.

Creative visualization can sustain and relax the couple as they make preparations for their wedding and marriage. It keeps them focused on happy results and gives them positive direction.

As the couple interact between themselves and with others, they can be aware of the areas of exchange most likely to produce stress.

Asserting One's Self

Many times, the bride and groom are inexperienced in negotiations to achieve their desired outcomes. The couple often finds it difficult to assert their rights or declare their wishes.

The bride reasons that the parents are paying for everything, so her desires are not worth mentioning. The supplier has been in business for a long time and must know the couple's desires better than they. The groom may hold back because the bride is so enthusiastic about her desires.

By lacking the assertiveness to make desires known, the ability to fulfill them is diminished. While the bride and groom must realize that each and every wish will not be met, they can be expressed. Once two or more are involved in a decision, compromise is always a possibility, but each person generally attempts to achieve all or most of their desires. The desires can be clearly announced in an attempt to accomplish them or mold them into a result that would be acceptable to many.

Love, friendship, or the service of others rarely produces mind reading capability. If the bride or the groom desires something, they must assert their wishes to each other and to those around them.

Building Self-esteem

Lack of assertiveness results from more than inexperience. It also results from a lack of self-esteem. A person may see any number of others as more deserving than themselves.

The bride may make excuses to herself as to why she let the honor attendant change the color scheme, or why she gave up the right to be married in the church she loves.

The groom reasons that it really isn't important that they drive off in a Rolls as he had envisioned. He may say he doesn't care about the guitar music he wanted during the ceremony, since it offends his future mother-in-law.

The individual verbally expresses the sentiment that it doesn't matter, but inwardly relays the message that he is not worthy. In her mind, she professes a lack of understanding and sees everyone else as more capable of making the right decision.

One should ask oneself the cause of low self-esteem and work toward raising their self-concept to the level of self acceptance and love. This exercise will help to assert one's desires and better interact with loved ones.

Healthy self-esteem also lets the individual realize that a desire may be rejected by a loved one. A refusal of a person's desire, however, is not a rejection of the person. Encountering opposition is not equal to meeting with humiliation or defeat.

Express Yourself

Compromise may be necessary, but elaboration or clarification of the desire may be all that is required. The more descriptive the bride or groom can be about their wants, the better others can understand and comply.

Good communication is a key element to interacting well with a spouse, children, parents, friends, and the community. The more skilled an individual becomes at clarifying thoughts and expressing them, the higher the quality of one's relationships.

The clearer the view one has of the future, and the clearer it is expressed to others, the less stress there will be as the individual makes the many changes that come with the challenges of living one's life.

11

Learning
to
Communicate

There is an ancient myth that at one point in time people had two heads, four arms and four legs, until they made the gods angry. In a ferocious rage, the people were split in two by the gods, and now people roam the earth seeking their other half.

It's very romantic to approach marriage with the thought of having found one's other half, and there are many times throughout the life of a husband and wife when it will be beneficial to act as one.

It's also important to be aware that realistically each person is marrying a whole individual. This individual has a history of their own, a communication style of their own, and values of their own. Your spouse-to-be has a unique style of experiencing anger and disappointment or joy and success.

How You See Yourself

Every person has an image of who they are and what it will mean to be married. The more clearly and confidently you see yourself and your future, the more successful you will be in communicating and negotiating what it is you want in your marriage and your life.

To be able to assert your desires, you must clearly understand the end result you wish to achieve. You need to feel worthy of attaining your goal and confident in your ability to achieve that which you desire.

A husband cannot rely on his wife to know and satisfy all his desires, just as the wife cannot expect her husband to be intuitively aware of and capable of fulfilling her every need.

Through discussions, commitment, and time, the two can learn to complement one another, while retaining their own individual personalities. But they will never respond to every situation life offers them as one. For, if during the marriage they are truly one individual, it can be certain that there is one individual and one mere shadow of a person.

Understanding Conversation

When any two people converse, there are three different levels of meaning occurring in the conversation:

First there is what the speaker is literally saying. Next there is the meaning the speaker believes those words are carrying to the listener, and finally there is the meaning the listener has attached to the words.

Previous discussions and past experiences will give meaning to the specific words. Because each individual comes to a marriage with a different history, it is possible to hear different meanings during the same discussion.

In Alice's family, her parents never used the words "I want". Instead they would phrase requests or demands as, "We will have to do better in school, Alice, or there will be no television." When a chore needed to be completed, her mother would tell her, "We must pick up the bedroom, Alice."

When Christopher and Alice began their marriage, past communication styles became a problem for them.

Chris worked at the bank until noon on Saturdays. As he was leaving for work, he would announce something like, "We have to go and do the laundry today, I'm out of shirts." Chris thought he was telling Alice that they had an afternoon project to accomplish together. Alice thought Chris was telling her to get the laundry finished while he was at work.

Afterward, Chris would express his gratitude to Alice for having finished the chores on her own, not realizing that Alice was seething about being slave labor.

Alice would coolly respond to Chris' "thank you", and proceed to sulk the remainder of the day. Alice could not tell him that she was overworked, because her parents would not have allowed her to complain.

It took the couple many unhappy months to realize that each gave different meaning to the same words.

There were several reasons for the couple's misunderstanding. One was that Alice did not value herself enough to say that she should not to be expected to do all of the chores alone. Her low level of self-esteem hindered her ability to assert that Chris was as responsible for the chores as she.

When Alice sulked about being burdened with the chores, Chris did not pursue the matter, but allowed time to work it out. He knew Alice was unhappy, but he hadn't a clue as to the cause.

When Chris was growing up, his father never verbally expressed his displeasure. If Chris had been disobedient, his father would stand before him, towering above Chris with his arms folded across his chest, anger causing his temples to bulge. His father would say nothing, but Chris knew he was in trouble.

Because of his history, Chris did not want to approach the silent, angered Alice, but rather kept his distance until she seemed less unhappy.

Response Awareness

The more aware a husband and wife can be to the response their communication elicits in the other, the sooner they can clarify their intentions. Often the expression on the other's face can be a clue that the words were not accepted by the listener as they were intended by the speaker. The nonverbal communication sent by the listener may be more clear than the verbal message sent by the speaker.

At that point, the speaker needs to ask the listener what was heard. This offers an immediate opportunity to rectify the situation in the present and to set new expectations for future conversations which are similar in nature.

Choosing the Right Words

Whenever people are communicating there is the possibility that the words they choose directly or indirectly indicate the value they have for another individual or an object.

The terms "my dear aunt" and "that old witch" clearly elicit different pictures in the listeners mind, and yet they may be used to describe the same person. It is the attitude the speaker has towards the person that leads to the choice of words.

It becomes more confusing when the same term is being used by two people, but the message being communicated is different. Take the word expensive, for instance. One item costing five hundred dollars may be called too expensive by some, while others wouldn't consider it expensive at all.

Patricia and Mark were having difficulty agreeing on the suppliers for their wedding. The couple had a limited budget and had decided to stretch their funds as far as was possible.

Patricia was beginning to feel that cuts in expenditures were only being made where she was concerned. She had wanted to limit the bridal party to three men and three women, reasoning that there would be fewer gifts to buy.

Mark had insisted that he had two additional friends he could not omit. When Patricia tried to include her young niece and nephew, however, Mark said that would be too expensive.

The gown Patricia chose was too expensive, and she had to settle for something less.

Mark chose a six-piece band, because in his estimation, the quality of the music made the party. Patricia thought they could hire a smaller band or a D.J.

The final straw came when Mark stated that the florist Patricia wanted to hire was too expensive. The flowers were important to her. She wanted numerous colors added to the church altar, bridal table, bouquets, and cake. She believed she had shopped well by finding a florist which met her needs at a very good price.

Mark argued that flowers just died. Patricia said the wedding was only one day anyway, and the flowers would appear in most of the photographs.

Before they had reached a decision on the florist. Mark informed Patricia that he was going to hire a Rolls Royce for the two of them. Of course, the Rolls was for the bride and groom only, so additional limousines would be necessary.

Patricia could not believe her ears. A Rolls Royce was not too expensive, but her flowers were too expensive. Patricia was frustrated and ready to cancel the wedding, as well as the marriage.

Fortunately, she was able to express to Mark what he was doing to her portion of the plans. By labeling those items he valued as being worth the price, and those only she valued as being expensive, he was depriving her of that which she wanted for their wedding. Until Patricia made him aware, Mark felt justified in the decisions he had made for the suppliers.

One of the reasons Patricia was successful in having Mark see her point of view was that she approached the discussion from her standpoint.

Patricia told Mark what she was experiencing as a result of his decisions, rather than accusing him of being unfair, or saying, "You are depriving me", she told him what she was experiencing as a result of his impact on their wedding plans.

Don't Assume

You are the only one who sees the world through your own eyes. Your perception will not be the perception of your partner or anyone else. Dealing with assumptions and pre-conceptions is a critical component in the crafting of a delightful wedding and a strong marital relationship.

You can state that you are experiencing discomfort or displeasure due to another's attitudes, demands, or decisions. You may then ask for the other's perception of the situation. This approach eliminates assumptions, produces compromise, and results in mutual happiness.

Compromise can arrive from a change in the situation, which requires the cooperation of the other individual, or from a change in attitude. A change in attitude is governed completely by the individual; one's own attitude is the only aspect of a relationship over which each person has complete control.

Because the bride and groom have enough in common to enter a marriage, they often assume their needs are identical. They may approach every discussion with the idea that their objectives are the same, only to discover later that one was experiencing discomfort, defeat, or anger at their perception that their special, personal needs were not being met.

Katie had a need to be extremely organized in every aspect of her life. When it came time to plan her marriage to Rob, she took on the task of wedding planning with the same organizational skills she had developed for every aspect of her life.

In addition to being organized, Katie was truly enjoying the preparations for the wedding. She probably shopped for twice as many suppliers than was actually necessary, but she was enjoying herself.

Rob, on the other hand, could not understand the need to make such a production out of their wedding plans. He became more irritable with each week that passed.

Katie would spend each evening on the commuter, jotting notes and planning strategy. Rob would pick her up at the train station, where she greeted him with her list of accomplishments, appointments, and tasks which still needed to be performed.

They would grab a quick dinner, and go off to meet with one o the suppliers. It was getting to the point where Rob didn't even want to meet Katie at the end of the work day.

Katie was having fun, and she was assuming Rob was doing the same. It wasn't until Rob started working late almost every evening that the two of them discussed what was occurring in their relationship.

In addition to projecting one's needs or goals onto the other. Individuals often project their feelings onto another.

Margie was perturbed with herself for spending more than they had budgeted for her wedding gown.

When she confronted Dan with the fact that she had overspent, she told him that she knew he was angry with her.

Kevin was having no success selling real estate. He wondered if he belonged in the sales profession. He confronted Mary with the idea that she thought he was a failure and wanted to cancel their wedding.

In both their cases, one partner was assuming how the other was feeling or reacting. In both cases the assumption was wrong.

It is presumptuous to assume one can read another's mind. Projecting the impression that one can is a very good way to kill a discussion or turn it into an argument.

Controlling Arguments

There are a number of ways people destroy the opportunity to better understand one another through discussion, allowing words to escalate into an argument or battle where one must be the victor and the other the conquered.

Fighting unfairly brings no positive results to the difference, but instead makes one or both persons more unhappy.

One such behavior which turns a discussion to a fight is to continuously interrupt the other person. This keeps one partner from making any points, jumbles his thinking, and irritates his disposition.

Finishing a sentence for the other person also prevents the other side of the difference from being told.

Mocking what one has just said only serves to anger the person, as does name calling and judgments.

Digging up the past also keeps the discussion from coming to any positive conclusions. It is difficult and confusing to deal with the past and the present simultaneously.

When one person becomes silent, refusing to further the discussion or argument there is no positive result. The same is true when one person walks from the room.

All of these fighting tactics serve only one of the partners. The tactics give one party control of the situation, but do not allow for a resolution of the disagreement.

One may have the attitude that the battle is won, but in fact, both have lost another opportunity to understand one another and correct their differences.

A more productive way to end a disagreement is to take one difference at a time, and remain with the present difference only. Each individual needs to describe their sense of the problem, without assuming they already know the other's perceptions and without laying blame for the situation.

Each person must state specifically what they want the end result to be, and what they are willing to do to achieve the result. Each needs to take responsibility for their own thoughts and feelings.

Finally, it is important throughout the discussion to ask what the other person understood the speaker to say.

Neither the husband nor the wife is perfect. Each will make mistakes throughout their marriage. Conflicts will work to the benefit of both, if each individual takes responsibility for any mistakes, learns from them, and is willing to rectify any errors in judgment.

Each individual has the right to change their mind over time, or to say, "I don't know," or "I don't understand". Each must be the judge of their own thoughts and emotions, as well as take responsibility for them.

The Nagging Parent Within

During the course of discussion, each individual needs to be alert to the nagging parent within.

Ellen's mother controlled her throughout her childhood by making demands, judging her as inadequate, and offering guilt rather than love.

Even Ellen's wedding date was controlled by her mother. When her mother fell from a ladder and was confined to a wheelchair just weeks before the wedding, Ellen was forced to postpone her marriage. Ellen's mother said, "If you love your mother, you will let her enjoy your wedding day".

Ellen vowed never to be like her mother, but once she married Bill, she found herself falling into a similar pattern. Rather than discussing a difference with Bill, Ellen found herself saying things like, "You should be more careful about your appearance!" or "You should phone when you'll be late."

Instead of accomplishing her objective, Ellen provoked anger in Bill. He in turn became more obstinate, refusing to do as Ellen wished.

Absolute words like "never" and "always" also trigger anger. Not only do the words cause the recipient to become hostile, but they also communicate a judgment that is clearly one-sided.

Respecting the Private Self

No one wishes to be judged unfavorably and especially by the person they love. The couple need to build trust between each other to allow for open expression.

When one person's feelings or attitudes are met by negative judgments or opinions on a continual basis, they tend to keep that part of themselves hidden.

Each person has a public self. This is the side which is presented to coworkers, neighbors, some relatives and friends. Then there is a private self which is reserved for only the most trusted of family and friends. Each partner in a marriage must work to establish the environment which permits and encourages the other to be comfortable revealing their private self.

Expression of the private self is important within a loving relationship. It is the goal of every marriage to be able to be free to portray that private self. To be expressed freely, there must be trust between the couple that the private self will not be pre-judged, criticized, or condemned.

The private self is not to be used against the person or revealed by the partner to family or friends.

Tony's father died when he was only ten years old. Suddenly the child became the "man of the house." He believed he needed to be the strong one in the family, as his father had been.

Lynn was initially attracted to Tony's strong, silence. She found it an admirable male characteristic. Eventually, though, Lynn realized that Tony was keeping a part of himself from her.

He would lapse into periods of silence which he would not share with her. She knew something was occurring within him, but she could not penetrate his tough outer shell.

With persistence on Lynn's part and great reluctance on the part of Tony, the couple became involved in their church's Marriage Encounter group.

Through the group's weekends and Lynn's loving and gentle encouragement, Tony was finally capable of revealing his troubled private self.

He was able to say he was scared that his company's cutbacks would cause him to lose his job.

He was able to face his daughter's illness, with Lynn's help. He was able to face his fear that she would die.

By opening their private selves to one another, Lynn and Tony were able to depend on one another for strength in their times of trouble. The result was a stronger marriage and two healthier individuals.

Marriage Help

There are Marriage Encounter groups available through religious organizations which offer couples assistance in learning to open their hearts and thoughts to one another.

Most religious organizations offer their own support for marriage, or are affiliated with an area group. Religious leaders have information readily available to couples wishing to strengthen their marriages.

Often the officiant will require marriage counseling of some sort prior to the marriage. This may be one on one with the officiant, or the bride and groom may meet with another couple involved in engagement support, or they may attend an Engagement Encounter Weekend, Discovery Weekend, or when children are involved, a Blending Family Opportunity Weekend.

The success of any of these experiences is dependent on the participants' openness and honesty. At times, it is necessary for the individual to become open to oneself, because feelings are buried so deeply. The benefits of the program depend on the participants' willingness to examine themselves, trust their partners, and let their feelings flow.

Encounter groups offer various types of weekend experiences, monthly discussion groups, and occasional workshops.

Ability to communicate is not something with which an individual is born. The quality of communication is only as good as is the person's teachers and experiences.

The more aware that one's communication style is uniquely one's own, as are one's thoughts, the more effort to be expended to offer communication that penetrates the listeners' consciousness.

It is by questioning the meaning which has been sent, the meaning which was received, and the end result which is desired that a husband and wife can best communicate with one another. From that communication, they will build a strong marriage and a strong family.

*A*fterthought

Each partner's expectations for the future can be open to exploration and discussion. What are the dreams each wishes to fulfill? What major accomplishments are to be made and how are they to be financed? When will each retire from full-time employment, and what will be the source of income at that time?

Throughout the engagement, there will be a number of opportunities when many of these issues will be raised. If the couple are alert to these opportunities, they may use them to their benefit.

One of the most emotion and value laden issues, that of religion, will surface when discussing where the ceremony will take place. If there are religious differences, they will become apparent when the ceremony site is discussed.

If the religious affiliations of the couple are similar, planning the ceremony may offer the opportunity for each to express beliefs which are personally important. If they are different, the process can be used to arrive at an understanding of the strength of each other's beliefs and to ensure mutual respect for the other's faith.

Budgeting for the wedding will also lead to value-based discussion. Each individual will have first hand experience working with the other on this major spending project. This is an ideal time to discuss the use of credit cards, application for loans, reduced spending to stay within a budget, and a savings plan.

The engagement will precipitate intense family time

as well. Discussion of the importance of family ties, the amount of influence each family will have on the marriage, and the future of the couple's family will make themselves apparent throughout the planning period before the wedding.

The question of where the couple will reside after the wedding can lead to conversations regarding the amount of space required, whether to own or rent, the geographic location desired, and the division of labor within the household.

As the couple progress through their wedding planning, they are presented with the opportunity to build a solid foundation for their marriage. Each new experience on the way to matrimony can offer the couple new insight into each other's expectations, beliefs, and requirements.

Every time a new subject is broached, there is an opportunity to learn and improve communication skills. The couple can learn to share the conversation, asking one another what was said or what was heard, clarifying any misunderstanding along the way.

Each can learn to be fair with the use of words, choice of topics, and expression of disagreement. Each can learn to offer the end result which they wish to achieve and explain what they are willing to do to achieve that goal.

With the clear direction of a goal and the possibility of its accomplishment, the couple can learn to compromise ambitions and develop a solution satisfactory to both.

Celebrating the wedding day is not an end result, but one step of an ongoing process. The wedding day preparations present an opportune time to learn a number of skills that the couple will require to see them through the numerous changes each will experience uniquely and together over the years.

$\mathcal{I}$ndex

A

Addressing invitations, 61-62, 105
Attendants
dance, 135
duties, 56-58
introduction of, 139-140
seating of, 139

B

Banquet facilities, 91-92
Beverages,alcoholic, 135
Birdseed, 89
Bouquet, throwing, 143
Bridal gown, 80-83, 97-99
Bridal table, 139

C

Cake, wedding,79, 106-107, 142-143
Candid photographs, 78
Caterer, 93
Children
as guests, 61-64
informing of marriage, 24-25
attendants, 129-130
in remarriage, 155
Classical music, 122

D

Dance, first, 134-135
Disabled persons, 91

E

Enclosures, invitation, 105-106
Engagement announcement
bride's parents, 14-15, 18-20
children, 24-25
divorced parents, 22
ex-spouse, 25
family/friends, 22-23
groom's parents, 20-21
newspaper, 25-26
public, 22-23, 25-26 28-29
Engagement
cancellation, 31-32, 151-152
formal proposal, 13-14
parental opinion, 17-18, 20, 32-34
party, 23
sibling rivalry, 29-32
Expenses, responsibility for, 48-50

F

Flowers, 83, 99-101, honored guest, 101
traditions, 101

wedding cake, 100-101

Food, 47-48, 67, 91,135-136

G

Garter, throwing, 143

Guest
children, 61-64
departure, 143-144
honored, 101
participation, 124-125
unwanted, 60-61

Guest list, 58-61

H

Horse and carriage, 108

Hymns, 122

I

Introductions, 139-140

Invitations. *See* Wedding invitations

M

Mailing invitations, 105

Marriage
communmication, 39, 41, 125, 170, 172-183
finances, 19, 36-38, 150-153
in-laws, 40-41
parental example, 27-28, 38-39

Marriage Encounter, 183

O

Officiant, 88, 89-90, 113, 116, 117,119, 120-121, 126,183

P

Parents
cake cutting, 142
dance, 134-135
divorced, 149-150
expenses, 49-50, 54
groom's, 53
hostess, 58
introduction, 21, 139-140
jealousy, 147,149-150
opinion of. *See* Engagement, Parental opinion
planning wedding, 46-47,165
processional, 118-119
receiving line, 126-127
title for, 40-41

Parents' table, 139

Photographs
candid, 78
montage, 96
photo-journalistic, 95
posed, 77-78, 94-95

Popular music, 121-122

R

Readings, 123-124

Receiving line, 126-127
Reception events
  bouquet throwing,
    143
  cake cutting, 142-143
  dance schedule, 134-
    135
  departure, 143-144
  garter throwing, 143
  introductions, 140-
    141
  prayer, 140-141
  receiving line, 126-
    127
  toast, 141
Religious holidays, 111
Remarriage. *See*
  Second marriage
Rental hall, 93
Response card, 62-63
  105-106

S
Scripture readings, 123
Second marriage, 24,
    82, 85, 114-115,
    138, 154-155, 155,
    155-156
Secular readings, 123-
    124
Seating arrangements,
    139
Supplier
  contract, 73-74, 76-
    77, 87, 91-92, 94,
    96, 100, 102-103,
    108

communications with,
    74-75,78-80
fees, 88, 90, 99, 108
interviews, 72-74, 90,
    99, 120
references, 71, 74,
    91, 104, 109

T
Traditional music, 121

V
Video, 96-97
Vocalist, 101-102

W
Wedding
  atmosphere, 131-132
  budget, 20, 29-31, 42,
    43-44, 47,150-153
  ceremony facility, 87,
    89, 112-114
  consultant, 103-104
  dance schedule, 134-
    135
  formality, 67, 137-
    139
  invitations, 61-62, 67,
    104-105, 131, 132,
    138
  music, 83-84, 90, 101-
    103, 121-122,
    133-135
  nontraditional, 44,
    51, 84-86, 138, 156-
    157
  organist, 90, 101

processional, 118-
    119, 166-167
program, 84, 127-128
reception facility, 90-
    93
religious require-
    ments, 65, 88-90,
    110-117
timetable, 66-67, 97,
toast, 141
Wedding, visualize, 42-
    46, 168-169, 172
Wedding hostess, 64,
    88-89

About the Author

Cynthia Kreuger, a bridal consultant/wedding coordinator, owns and, operates White Lace Bridal Services, Ltd. Writing her newspaper column, "Proposals ... Advice for the Bride-to-Be", as well as operating her referral and coordinating service, keeps her in constant communication with engaged couples, their families, and wedding suppliers.

Available from Brighton Publications, Inc.

Wedding Occasions: 101 New Party Themes for Wedding Showers, Rehearsal Dinners, Engagement Parties, and More! by Cynthia Lueck Sowden

Games for Wedding Shower Fun by Sharon Dlugosch, Florence Nelson

Wedding Plans: 50 Unique Themes for the Wedding of Your Dreams by Sharon Dlugosch

Wedding Hints & Reminders by Sharon Dlugosch

Folding Table Napkins by Sharon Dlugosch

Table Setting Guide by Sharon Dlugosch

Tabletop Vignettes by Sharon Dlugosch

Games for Party Fun by Sharon Dlugosch

Christmas Party Celebrations: 71 New and Exciting Party Plans for Holiday Fun by Denise Distel Dytrych

Reunions for Fun-Loving Families by Nancy Funke Bagley

An Anniversary to Remember: Years One to Seventy-Five by Cynthia Lueck Sowden

Romantic At-Home Dinners: Sneaky Strategies for Couples with Kids by Nan Booth/Gary Fischler

Kid-Tastic Birthday Parties: The Complete Party Planner for Today's Kids by Jane Chase

Baby Shower Fun by Sharon Dlugosch

Games for Baby Shower Fun by Sharon Dlugosch

Don't Slurp Your Soup: A Basic Guide to Business Etiquette by Elizabeth Craig

Hit the Ground Running: Communicate Your Way to Business Success by Cynthia Kreuger

Installation Ceremonies for Every Group: 26 Memorable Ways to Install New Officers by Pat Hines

Meeting Room Games: Getting Things Done in Committees by Nan Booth

These books are available in selected stores. If you need help finding them in your area, send a self-addressed, stamped, business-size envelope or call to request ordering information:

Brighton Publications, Inc.
P.O. Box 120706
St. Paul, MN 55112-0706

1-800-536-BOOK (2665)   http://www.partybooks.com